THIRD EDITION

ESTATE
DREAM HOMES

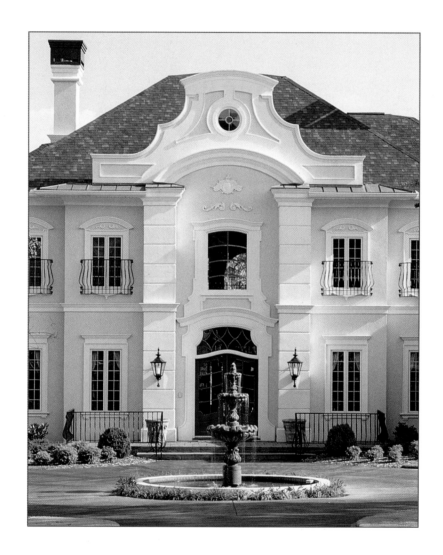

181 DESIGNS
OF
UNSURPASSED GRANDEUR

HOME PLANNERS, LLC
Wholly owned by Hanley-Wood, LLC

Tucson, Arizona
www.eplans.com

ESTATE DREAM HOMES

Published by Home Planners, LLC
Wholly owned by Hanley-Wood, LLC
3275 W. Ina Road, Suite 110
Tucson, Arizona 85741

Distribution Center:
29333 Lorie Lane
Wixom, Michigan 48393

Jayne Fenton, *President*
Jennifer Pearce, *Vice President, Group Content*
Linda Bellamy, *Executive Editor*
Jan Prideaux, *Editor in Chief*
Arlen Feldwick-Jones, *Editorial Director*
Vicki Frank, *Managing Editor*
Kristin Schneidler, *Editor*
Jill Hall, *Plans Editor*
Chester E. Hawkins, *Creative Manager*
Paul Fitzgerald, *Senior Graphic Designer*
William Knight, *Graphic Production Artist*
Sara Lisa, *Senior Production Manager*
Brenda McClary, *Production Manager*

Photo Credits
Front Cover: Design HPT800123; see page 155. Photo by Dave Dawson,
design by ©Stephen Fuller, Inc.
Back Cover: Design by ©Home Design Services, Inc.
Page 4: Photo ©Laurence Taylor Photography, courtesy of
The Sater Design Collection.
©2002 by Home Planners, LLC

10 9 8 7 6 5 4 3 2 1

Printed in the United States of America

Library of Congress Catalog Card Number: 2001095318
ISBN softcover: 1-931131-00-7

CONTENTS

EDITOR'S NOTE

GRAND, LUXURIOUS HOMES ARE MADE

to stand the test of time, but the needs and desires of homebuyers can change in just a few years. Architects and designers work to adapt their creations to today's new technologies and active lifestyles, and, to keep up with the times, we've also adapted one of our best collections. The third edition of Estate Dream Homes— fully revised, updated and drawn from the portfolios of 18 celebrated designers— is filled with plans that honor the past but live in the present.

"Barefoot Elegance" introduces designs—of every shape and style—that combine the formal, well-loved details of grand estates with the best elements of today's family homes. Libraries and music rooms, surrounded by high ceilings and sweeping staircases, join cozy dens, welcoming hearth or keeping rooms and high-tech media rooms. Looking for a breezy, carefree estate for the seaside or lakefront that you call home? The plans that fill the "On the Waterfront" collection blend airy informality with luxurious amenities, and offer plenty of courtyards, porches and verandas to take in the view. The homes of "Old World Splendor" capture the grace and dignity of grand European estates, both past and present, with sturdy brick and stone facades sure to maintain their timeless beauty. And "A Place in the Sun" showcases a variety of fine Mediterranean-style estates, with soaring arches, brilliant stucco facades and sparkling expanses of glass.

The estate plans found here are a memorable group—dramatic yet refined, unsurpassed in grandeur yet filled with the comforts that reassure us, and fully inspirational. But this collection is not meant only to inspire—the designs in this book are intended to be built and enjoyed for years to come. Find the one that's right for you, and start the process of creating your own estate dream home.

A massive stone hearth is the focal point of the great room; another enticing feature is the hardwood floor.

ON THE WATERFRONT

*Rustic accents add charm to this
resort-style estate*

DESIGN HPT800001

Bring luxurious resort-style living into your life with this spacious design. An intriguing blend of architectural details—a Craftsman-style front gable, appealing dormers above the garage and plenty of tall windows—draws the eye to the exterior, while the interior offers today's most-wanted amenities.

A central great room, enhanced by an exposed-beam ceiling, fireplace and wet bar, is the heart of this comfortable estate. A wall of windows brings natural light to this room, which overlooks the media/recreation room in the basement. To the left of the great room, informal columns define the dining room, which opens to a charming gourmet kitchen with a pantry, an island cooktop and a box-bay window over the double sink. The screened porch, also accessible through the dining room, includes a second fireplace and opens to side and rear covered porches. Both the dining room and screened porch feature soaring cathedral ceilings. To the right of the great room, the study/sitting area includes a third fireplace.

Sleeping quarters on the first level, shielded from the main traffic areas by the study/sitting room, include a master suite and two family bedrooms. Highlights in the master suite include a columned entry and cathedral ceiling in the bedroom, and a soaking tub, separate shower and built-in cabinetry in the private bath—a walk-in closet can be reached through the bath as well. The two family bedrooms, brightened by multiple windows, share a bath/shower area; each has a private toilet and vanity sink.

Downstairs, the expansive media/recreation room, warmed by the home's fourth fireplace, includes a wet bar and opens to a covered patio area. Two more bedrooms, each with a private bath, flank this central room; one of the bedrooms even includes a walk-in closet and opens to another covered patio. A large storage area completes the plan.

Left: Tucked into a corner of the great room, the warm browns of this furniture collection set a relaxed mood. Below: Wicker furnishings and a wrought-iron fireplace screen lend a comfortably rustic air to the screened porch. Bottom: Picture windows provide panoramic views in the master bedroom, where the cool green tones and hardwood floors echo the natural shades just outside the windows.

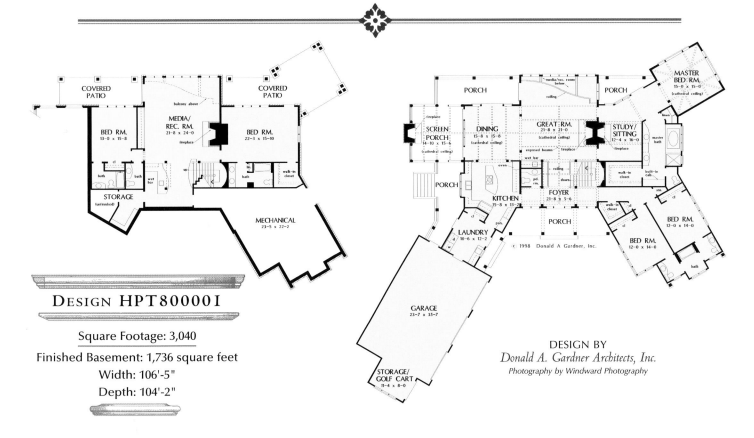

COVERED PATIO

BED RM.
13-0 x 15-8

MEDIA/ REC. RM.
21-8 x 24-0

balcony above

fireplace

COVERED PATIO

BED RM.
22-3 x 15-10

wet bar

STORAGE
(unfinished)

walk-in closet

MECHANICAL
23-5 x 22-2

PORCH

media/rec. room below

railing

PORCH

MASTER BED RM.
15-0 x 15-0
(cathedral ceiling)

fireplace

SCREEN PORCH
14-10 x 15-6
(cathedral ceiling)

DINING
15-8 x 15-8
(cathedral ceiling)

GREAT RM.
21-8 x 21-0
(cathedral ceiling)

exposed beams

STUDY/ SITTING
12-4 x 16-0

fireplace

linen

master bath

wet bar

PORCH

KITCHEN
15-8 x 13-2

oven

pd. rm.

railing

down

walk-in closet

built-in cab.

FOYER
21-8 x 5-6

walk-in closet

BED RM.
12-0 x 14-0

PORCH

LAUNDRY
10-6 x 12-2

w

d

© 1998   Donald A Gardner, Inc.

BED RM.
12-0 x 14-0

bath

GARAGE
23-7 x 35-7

STORAGE/ GOLF CART
11-4 x 8-0

Design HPT80000I

Square Footage: 3,040

Finished Basement: 1,736 square feet

Width: 106'-5"

Depth: 104'-2"

DESIGN BY
Donald A. Gardner Architects, Inc.
Photography by Windward Photography

This home, as shown in the photographs, may differ from the actual blueprints.
For more detailed information, please check the floor plans carefully.

Built-in cabinetry, a tub big enough for two and great outdoor views offer luxury in the master bath.

OLD WORLD SPLENDOR

An elegant entry, a wrought-iron balcony and a stone-and-brick facade establish this estate's European character

DESIGN HPT800002

This magnificent home is created with complete elegance and sophistication in mind. The gracefully flared eaves complement the solid brick and stone exterior of this facade. The amazing balcony from the second-story bedroom and the beautifully etched front door are just a few of the wonderful details found in this home. Tall windows accentuate the airiness and openness of this home. Spacious and open rooms make this home ideal for entertaining, whether it is a formal or not-so-formal get-together. A spectacular pub is conveniently located between the kitchen and the great

Above: The deep red bricks are accented well by the bright gray stone on this marvelous facade.

room for all entertaining and serving purposes. The bar adds a definite detail of excitement to this home. A cozy dining area can also be placed in the pub for those intimate but informal occasions. A warming hearth makes the great room a comfortable area for family and friends year round. The open plan also allows the view of the hearth to be enjoyed from various rooms in the home. An island adds extra counter space to the already roomy kitchen, so that no matter how large the gathering, this home can accommodate. The elegant French doors lead to the library, which is well lit by the grand window. The laundry room is well situated near the kitchen and off the garage.

The luxurious sleeping quarters feature the master suite, which is located on the first level, and three family bedrooms, which are located on the second level. The lush master suite showcases dual vanities, a spacious walk-in closet and tray ceilings. Two of the bedrooms on the second level feature walk-in closets, while one offers elegant French doors to an elongated closet. A balcony dresses up one of the bedrooms wonderfully.

Left: The cream colored window dressing, couch and chair delicately contrast the dark wooden end tables, coffee table and piano. Below: Dark woods, gently illuminated by an elegant chandelier, accent the dining room as well.

The elegant marble bar works well in contrast with the casual wooden cabinetry and chairs.

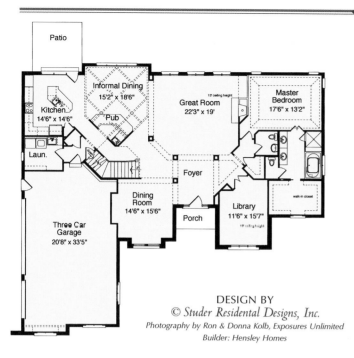

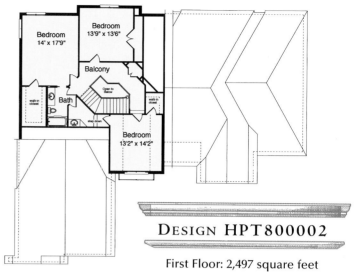

DESIGN BY
© *Studer Residental Designs, Inc.*
Photography by Ron & Donna Kolb, Exposures Unlimited
Builder: Hensley Homes

DESIGN HPT800002

First Floor: 2,497 square feet
Second Floor: 1,167 square feet
Total: 3,664 square feet

Width: 72'-4"
Depth: 65'-0"

This home, as shown in the photographs, may differ from the actual blueprints.
For more detailed information, please check the floor plans carefully.

*A comfortable atmosphere
is set in the pub by the
wooden coffered ceiling
and hardwood floor*

The grand room is an opulent retreat, providing a French salon atmosphere.

BAREFOOT ELEGANCE

Luxurious yet comfortable, these two estates move
gracefully between formal and casual

DESIGN HPT800180

Reminiscent of an English country manor, this innovative design reflects stately Georgian elegance and provides an ultra-chic floor plan. A columned covered porch and divided-light windows enhance the front view of the home. In the foyer, a breathtakingly beautiful circular staircase with a wrought-iron railing makes a dashing first impression. Wide-plank oak flooring, which warms the first floor as well as the second-floor hall, complements the extensive custom woodwork and trim used throughout the home.

Beyond the gallery hall, the grand room provides a highly decorated French salon atmosphere. Furnished with silver-and-gold-leaf silk upholstery, damasks and velvets, the living space creates a seating area that invites great events, yet is comfortable enough for casual gatherings. To the left of the plan, a lavish banquet hall offers a plush and enchanting environment.

The bright breakfast bay leads to a private area of the rear deck, which also opens from the living areas and the master suite. A 17th-Century fireplace warms this casual gathering area. An equestrian theme creates a perfect ambiance in the family room, with provincial paintings and deep leather-upholstered sofas. The adjacent kitchen boasts custom-crafted cabinets, plus plenty of counter space. A side staircase leads to a finished basement, which in this design takes on the appearance of a log cabin, with stucco and wainscotting, and pine-paneled "log" walls. This cabin-like space is also a gaming retreat, with an oversized bar, billiard room, media center and jukebox. A stunning master retreat features shades of chocolate brown with cream and ivory, elegantly mixed with more feminine furnishings, accessories and fabrics. A sunken marble whirlpool tub highlights the bath. The suite also offers a sitting area, which accesses a rear-covered terrace.

Upstairs, a charming balcony overlooks the grand room. The entertainment/computer loft is a busy area, which offers a state-of-the-art home theater, while the 21st-Century high-tech office is complete with up-to-the-minute components. Three family bedrooms offer private baths and walk-in closets.

Left: The breathtaking circular staircase is gracefully accented by wrought-iron railing. Right: The exquisite banquet hall provides a lavish dining experience for any occasion. Far Right: The open kitchen boasts custom-crafted cabinets and extensive counter space.

DESIGN HPT800180

First Floor: 2,756 square feet
Second Floor: 1,631 square feet
Finished Basement: 1,576 square feet
Total: 5,963 square feet

Width: 75'-0"
Depth: 65'-4"

DESIGN BY
© *Garrell Associates, Inc*
Photography by Visual Solutions Co.
and © Peter Fownes

This home, as shown in the photographs, may differ from the actual blueprints.
For more detailed information, please check the floor plans carefully.

DESIGN HPT800003

Corinthian columns announce an inviting entry, rich with panels of leaded glass. Marble columns with gilded accents frame a sweeping staircase in the foyer, which opens to the formal dining hall and the grand salon. A bow window brings in plenty of light and a sense of nature, while a massive fireplace anchors this voluminous living space. French doors open to a covered veranda—a very nice arrangement for planned occasions.

A vivid palette warms the keeping room and plays counterpoint to natural light and the soothing colors of the Arcadian grove outside. Open to the morning nook and kitchen, the keeping room shares the glow of its hearth with the casual eating areas. Well-organized amenities such as an angled cooktop, dual food-preparation islands and a walk-in pantry facilitate even crowd-size events.

Rich with hardwood panels and secluded behind French doors, this private room allows repose for the homeowners. Connected to the master suite by a vestibule that leads to the master bath, the library easily serves as an extension of the homeowner's retreat. Spectacular arches define the bedroom, and French doors open the space to the veranda.

Rich marble and gilded columns announce the living space.

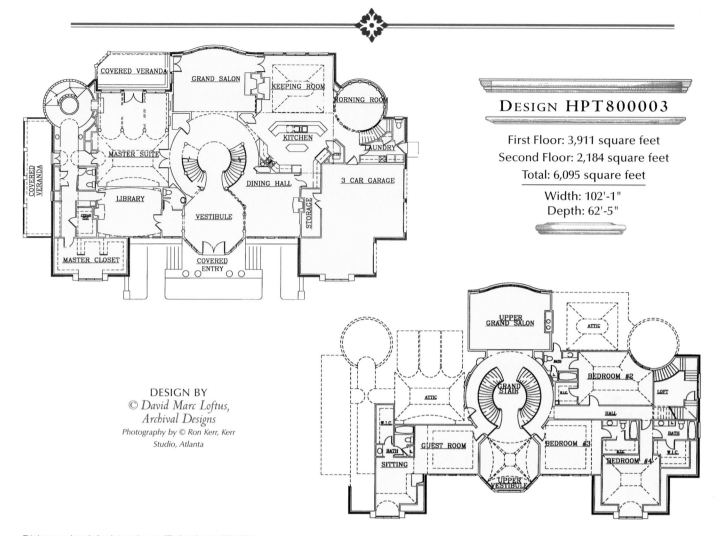

DESIGN HPT800003

First Floor: 3,911 square feet
Second Floor: 2,184 square feet
Total: 6,095 square feet

Width: 102'-1"
Depth: 62'-5"

DESIGN BY
© *David Marc Loftus,*
Archival Designs
Photography by © Ron Kerr, Kerr
Studio, Atlanta

This home, as shown in the photographs, may differ from the actual blueprints.
For more detailed information, please check the floor plans carefully.

Neutral shades create a sophisticated look in the living room, which enjoys an expansive view of the pool.

A PLACE IN THE SUN

*Two opulent Floridian designs showcase
the best of today's estate features*

DESIGN HPT800176

This awe-inspiring Sun Country home features sublime Palladian and gloriously arched windows. Decoratively detailed columns blend into the keystone and lintel arches that elegantly display the entryway. The beautiful stucco exterior matched with the classic shingled rooftop creates the luxurious Floridian style showcased here. French doors lead to the foyer, which faces the angled living room; wonderfully high ceilings and fantastic views from the backyard make this room both soothing and entertaining. A fireplace can be found in the living room for maximum comfort—no matter what the season. The open dining room also features high ceilings and tall windows. The family study has plenty of room for office space as well as a splendid library. The gracious breakfast nook is conveniently located near the leisure room and the kitchen serves both rooms exquisitely with an island and extra preparation space. Views from the veranda can be enjoyed from each of the rooms facing the backyard. The bright windows from the leisure room and breakfast nook enliven the kitchen with tons of natural light. An outdoor kitchen also relishes in sunlight and is perfect for outdoor gatherings.

A Place in the Sun

The extravagant sleeping areas begin with the lavish, amenity-filled master suite. French doors open into this suite, where a bayed sitting area and sliding doors off the veranda allow natural light to enter. Two spacious walk-in closets offer plenty of wardrobe space and are located between the bed and the bath, where dual vanities and access to a privacy garden are available. Two family bedrooms are also found on the first floor; another is located on the second floor, along with a loft. Each bedroom offers its own bath and walk-in closet. French doors open to the bedroom on the second floor, while the rear bedroom on the first floor has private access to the rear veranda. All bedrooms are filled with extras for the whole family.

Decorative ceiling details add spectacular style to this elegant master suite.

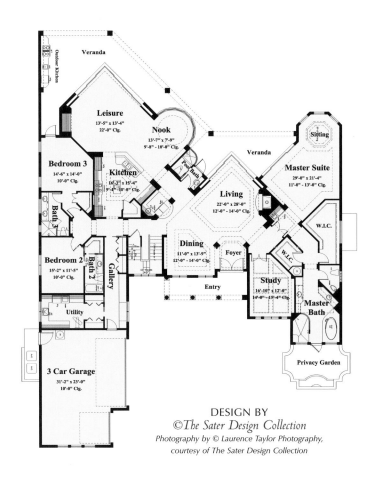

Veranda

Outdoor Kitchen

Leisure
13'-5" x 13'-4"
22'-0" Clg.

Nook
13'-7" x 7'-9"
9'-8" - 10'-0" Clg.

Sitting

Veranda

Master Suite
29'-0" x 21'-4"
11'-0" - 13'-0" Clg.

Bedroom 3
14'-6" x 14'-0"
10'-0" Clg.

Kitchen
16'-3" x 15'-4"
9'-4" - 10'-0" Clg.

Pool Bath

Living
22'-0" x 28'-0"
12'-0" - 14'-0" Clg.

Bath 3

Dining
11'-0" x 13'-9"
12'-0" - 14'-0" Clg.

Foyer

Bedroom 2
15'-2" x 11'-5"
10'-0" Clg.

Bath 2

Gallery

Entry

W.I.C.

W.I.C.

Utility

Study
16'-10" x 12'-0"
14'-0" - 15'-4" Clg.

Master Bath

3 Car Garage
31'-2" x 23'-0"
10'-0" Clg.

Privacy Garden

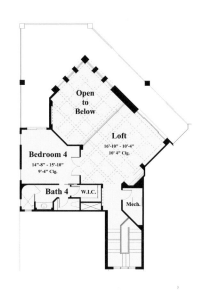

Open to Below

Loft
16'-10" - 10'-4"
10' 4" Clg.

Bedroom 4
14'-8" - 15'-10"
9'-4" Clg.

Bath 4

W.I.C.

Mech.

DESIGN BY
©The Sater Design Collection
Photography by © Laurence Taylor Photography,
courtesy of The Sater Design Collection

DESIGN HPT800176

First Floor: 4,137 square feet
Second Floor: 876 square feet
Total: 5,013 square feet

Width: 81'-10"
Depth: 113'-0"

This home, as shown in the photographs, may differ from the actual blueprints.
For more detailed information, please check the floor plans carefully.

A dome is built over the veranda and pool area to make this home perfect for every form of outdoor entertaining, no matter what the weather.

Design HPT800177

Keystone arches, tall windows and elegant columns accent the exterior of this impressive Floridian design. Its subdued stucco facade, paired with a tiled roof, blends well with the landscape. A charming brick walkway leads to the front entry, where double doors open to a foyer with a soaring ceiling.

Living spaces, both formal and informal, are centrally located. Just beyond the foyer, the dining room and study—both with eye-catching ceiling treatments—flank the spacious living room. Both the dining room and study are open to the veranda, while a curved wall of glass in the living room provides views of the rear property. The gourmet kitchen, featuring a center island, wrapping counters and a walk-in pantry, adjoins a cozy breakfast nook. A fireplace and a pyramid vault ceiling make the leisure room—secluded to the rear of the plan—memorable, while sliding glass doors open to the veranda and a charming outdoor kitchen.

Left: A double-door, etched-glass entry, striking ceiling detail and tall, distinguished columns enhance the living room and foyer. Above: Palm trees and blue skies provide the perfect backdrop for this Floridian estate. Below: Warm woods, decorative pottery and gentle lighting make this corner of the kitchen a cozy spot.

Sleeping spaces are kept wonderfully private in this design. To the left of the plan, a gallery hall leads to two guest suites, each with a private bath and walk-in closet. The master suite, accessed through double doors, fills the right wing of the home. The master bedroom, with a private bay-window sitting area, tray ceiling and access to the veranda, provides a peaceful retreat, while the adjoining bath includes a raised oval tub set in a bay, two vanity areas and a compartmented toilet and bidet. A walk-in closet, made for convenience with built-in shelving, is accessible from both the bedroom and the bath.

Masterful outdoor lighting lends a warm, inviting glow to the veranda and pool.

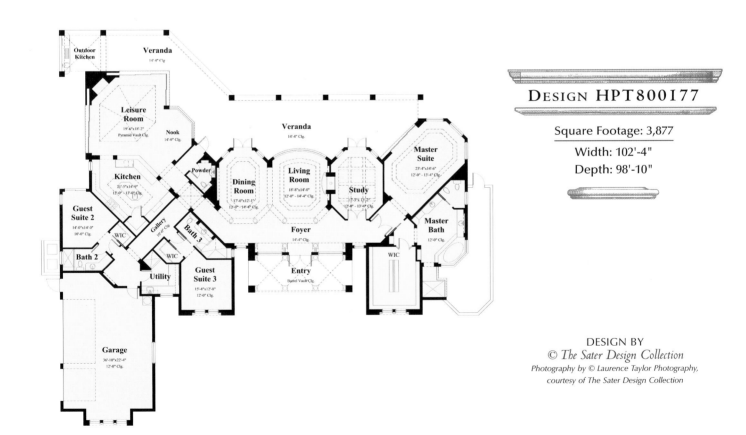

DESIGN HPT800177

Square Footage: 3,877

Width: 102'-4"
Depth: 98'-10"

DESIGN BY
© *The Sater Design Collection*
Photography by © Laurence Taylor Photography,
courtesy of The Sater Design Collection

Barefoot Elegance

Luxurious estates designed for carefree living

Design HPT800044, see page 73

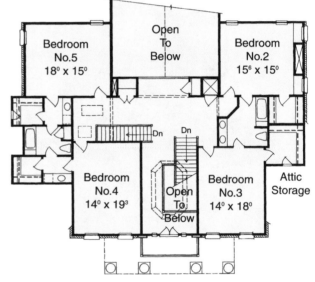

Bedroom No.5 18⁰ x 15⁰

Open To Below

Bedroom No.2 15⁶ x 15⁰

Bedroom No.4 14⁰ x 19³

Dn   Dn

Open To Below

Bedroom No.3 14⁰ x 18⁰

Attic Storage

DESIGN HPT800005

First Floor: 3,902 square feet

Second Floor: 2,159 square feet

Total: 6,061 square feet

Width: 85'-3"

Depth: 74'-0"

Screened Porch

Solarium 14⁰ x 15⁰

Kitchen 15³ x 17⁰

Breakfast 13³ x 15⁰

Family Room 22⁶ x 21⁶

Study 17⁶ x 14⁹

Up   Dn

Dining Room 14⁰ x 19³

Living Room 14⁰ x 22⁶

Master Bedroom 20⁶ x 17⁹

Foyer

Up

Three Car Garage 20⁶ x 33⁰

Porch

The entry to this classic home is framed with a sweeping double staircase and four large columns topped with a pediment. The two-story foyer is flanked by spacious living and dining rooms. Beyond the foyer, the home is designed with rooms that offer maximum livability. The two-story family room, which has a central fireplace, opens to the study and a solarium. A spacious U-shaped kitchen features a central island cooktop. An additional staircase off the breakfast room offers convenient access to the second floor. The impressive master suite features backyard access and a bath fit for royalty. A walk-in closet with an ironing board will provide room for everything. Four bedrooms upstairs enjoy large proportions. This home is designed with a walkout basement foundation.

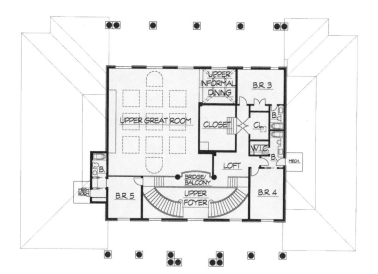

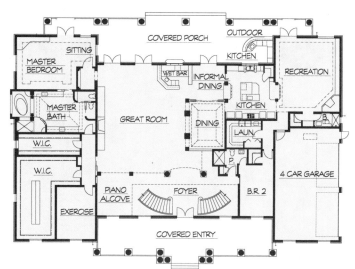

DESIGN HPT800006

First Floor: 6,713 square feet
Second Floor: 1,554 square feet
Total: 8,267 square feet

Width: 120'-4"
Depth: 88'-8"

This estate offers luxurious living in grand Greek Revival style. The interior begins with a foyer—a piano alcove is just to the left—defined by columns. Straight ahead, the great room features a fireplace and a wet bar, and borders both formal and informal dining areas. The island kitchen, where a double window overlooks a charming outdoor kitchen, includes a walk-in pantry; the nearby recreation area, with a second fireplace, opens to the covered rear porch. The master suite dominates the left wing and provides a sitting area, two huge walk-in closets, a lavish bath and an exercise room. Upstairs, three family bedrooms each have a private bath.

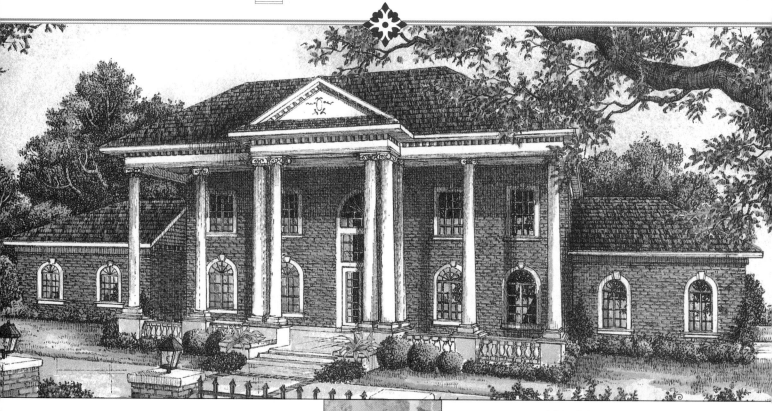

BAREFOOT ELEGANCE

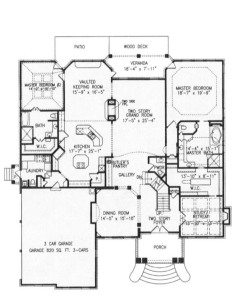

DESIGN HPT800007

First Floor: 3,364 square feet

Second Floor: 1,160 square feet

Total: 6,938 square feet

Finished Basement: 2,414 square feet

Storage Area: 1,288 square feet

Width: 69'-0"

Depth: 75'-0"

This imposing stone facade is full of grace and defined taste. An escalating front stairwell leads to elegant French doors. The two-story foyer is flanked by a dining room and study/retreat area—which is complete with a fireplace. A two-sided fireplace warms both the vaulted keeping room and the grand room, making entertaining a large group of guests entirely enjoyable. A butler's pantry is convenient to the dining room. The kitchen features a roomy island enabling serving to the keeping and grand rooms. The first floor also has two lavish master suites. Two family bedrooms, a balcony with a sun porch, two storage areas and an optional bonus room are located on the second story, making this a home of luxury and practicality.

Second floor plan:

BONUS RM.
28-2 x 13-0

attic storage

BED RM.
13-8 x 12-4
(vaulted ceiling)

BED RM.
13-8 x 12-4
(vaulted ceiling)

bath

bath

storage

attic storage

lin.

cl

foyer below

cl

family room below

railing

balcony

down

First Floor: 2,908 square feet
Second Floor: 790 square feet
Total: 3,698 square feet

Bonus Room: 521 square feet
Width: 86'-11"
Depth: 59'-5"

First floor plan:

GUEST
13-0 x 15-0

BRKFST.
13-4 x 12-9

PORCH

DECK

(two story ceiling)

fireplace

MASTER BED RM.
18-0 x 15-0

FAMILY RM.
24-4 x 16-6

fireplace

KITCHEN
14-0 x 16-6

balcony above

shelves

walk-in closet

UTILITY
11-4 x 6-0

shelves

DINING
14-0 x 13-0

FOYER
10-0 x 11-4

LIVING RM./ STUDY
14-0 x 13-8

master bath

lin.

GARAGE
22-0 x 24-0

PORCH

bath

d   w

pd. rm.

cl

up

A stately hip roof crowns this impressive executive home's brick exterior, which includes arch-topped windows, keystones and a covered entry with a balustrade. The spacious floor plan boasts formal and casual living areas. A two-story ceiling in the foyer and family room highlights an exciting curved balcony on the second floor. The kitchen is generously proportioned and includes a center island roomy enough for the kitchen sink and plenty of work space. Distinctive shelving is built into either end of the home's center hall. The master suite and a guest suite, each with tray ceilings and private baths, are located on the first floor. Two bedrooms with vaulted ceilings, two full baths and a bonus room can be found upstairs.

BAREFOOT ELEGANCE

DESIGN HPT800009

First Floor: 3,615 square feet

Second Floor: 1,066 square feet

Total: 4,681 square feet

Bonus Space: 979 square feet

Width: 90'-0"

Depth: 63'-0"

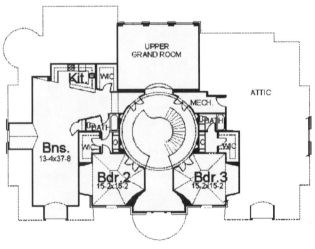

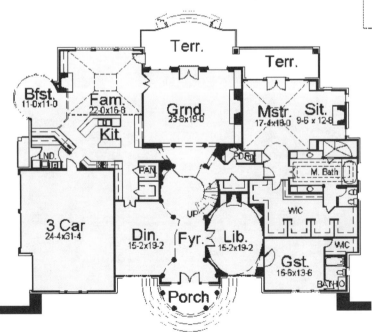

A sweeping central staircase is just one of the impressive features of this lovely estate home. Four fireplaces—in the library, family room, grand room and master-suite sitting room—add a warm glow to the interior; the master suite, grand room and family room all open to outdoor terrace space. There's plenty of room for family and guests—a guest suite sits to the front of the plan, joining the master suite and two more family bedrooms. Upstairs, a large bonus area—possibly a mother-in-law suite—offers a petite kitchen and walk-in closet; a full bath is nearby.

38   ESTATE DREAM HOMES

Floor Plans

Second Floor:

Bdr 2
14-2 x 13-4

BATH

WIC

UPPER GRND.

ATTIC

Stdo.
15-5 x 7-0

DN

WIC

DN

BATH

Bdr 3
13-7 x 16-1

UPPER FOYER

Bdr 4
13-7 x 15-2

BATH

Bns.
17-5 x 20-7

First Floor:

Deck

Fam.
19-4 x 18-0

Grnd.
17-0 x 19-8

Ver.

Mstr.
19-8 x 19-6

Morn.
11-0 x 12-0

Kit.
23-5 x 12-0

DN

WIC

M.BATH

LND.

PDR.

UP

WIC

3 Car
21-4 x 20-4

Din.
13-6 x 16-1

Fyr.

UP

Lib.
13-7 x 13-4

PORCH

DESIGN HPT800010

First Floor: 2,914 sq. ft.
Second Floor: 1,450 sq. ft.
Total: 4,364 sq. ft.

Width: 67'-8"
Depth: 70'-2"

Arched windows accent the sturdy brick exterior of this elegant design. The foyer, flanked by the formal dining hall and expansive library, offers dramatic views of the central staircase, followed by the grand salon. The left wing of the plan provides space for carefree family living–the hearth-warmed family room opens to a rear deck, a vaulted ceiling decorates the cozy morning room, and the island kitchen allows space for multiple cooks. The morning room brightens the area with natural morning sunlight. The master bedroom includes French door access to the rear patio. Three family bedrooms are located on the second level, each have separate baths and walk-in closets.

This family delight will be the most perfect home in the neighborhood. The expansive windows and pedimented arches create a majestic aura. The living room/study offers two choices for the family to spend its leisure time. The exposed beams, fireplace, and bay window all play a large role in the comfort bestowed here. The dining area is just steps from the kitchen, optimizing the servability function for those informal and formal nights of entertaining. The ribbon of windows in the breakfast nook enlivens the kitchen. The family room borders the rear porch and offers a great place to spend time in front of the warming hearth. The master suite has a walk-in closet, access to the back porch, and a compartmented bath with double-bowl vanity. Three family bedrooms and a loft are located on the second level. Each bedroom is complete with a walk-in closet.

DESIGN HPT800011

First Floor: 2,330 square feet

Second Floor: 1,187 square feet

Total: 3,517 square feet

Width: 90'-2"
Depth: 47'-2"

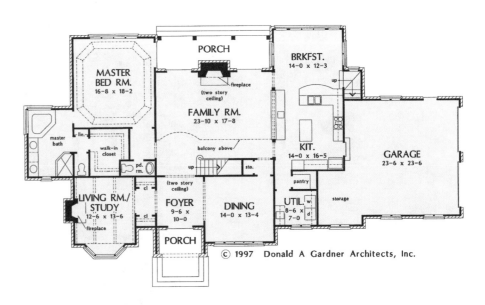

© 1997 Donald A Gardner Architects, Inc.

PORCH

MASTER BED RM.
16-0 x 18-0

master bath

walk-in closet

master bath

walk-in closet

GREAT RM.
27-8 x 21-8
(14' ceiling)

fireplace

BRKFST.
18-0 x 11-0

SUN RM.
14-0 x 14-0

PORCH

pantry

KIT.
18-0 x 19-4

BED RM.
13-10 x 13-0

walk-in closet   cl

walk-in closet   cl

STUDY
12-8 x 14-6
(12' ceiling)

FOYER
8-9 x 11-0
(12' ceiling)

down   up

shelves

cl

pd. rm.

wet bar

DINING
13-10 x 17-2
(14' ceiling)

bath

cl

UTILITY
12-1 x 11-4

STORAGE
9-6 x 11-4

d   w

bath

BED RM.
14-0 x 13-0

PORCH

BED RM.
14-8 x 14-0

sto.

GARAGE
23-0 x 33-8

Large and rambling, this four-bedroom home is sure to please every member of the family. The homeowner will especially appreciate the master bedroom suite. Here, luxuries such as His and Hers bathrooms, two walk-in closets and a tray ceiling await to pamper. For gatherings, the spacious great room lives up to its name, with a fireplace, built-ins, a tray ceiling and access to the rear porch. The kitchen features an island cooktop/snack bar, a walk-in pantry and an adjacent bayed breakfast room. A sun room is also nearby. Note the storage in the three-car garage.

DESIGN HPT800012

Square Footage: 4,523

Width: 114'-4"
Depth: 82'-3"

DESIGN HPT800013

First Floor: 2,603 square feet

Second Floor: 1,020 square feet

Total: 3,623 square feet

Width: 76'-8"

Depth: 68'-0"

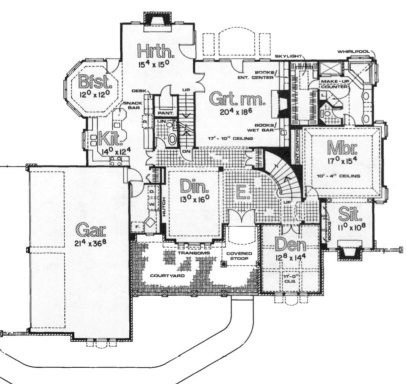

Perhaps the most notable characteristic of this traditional house is its masterful use of space. The glorious great room, open dining room and handsome den serve as the heart of the home. A cozy hearth room with a fireplace rounds out the kitchen and breakfast area. The master bedroom opens up to a private sitting room with a fireplace. Three family bedrooms occupy the second floor, each one with a private bath. Other special features include a four-car garage, a corner whirlpool tub in the master bath, a walk-in pantry and snack bar in the kitchen, and transom windows in the dining room.

DESIGN HPT800014

First Floor: 2,813 square feet
Second Floor: 1,091 square feet
Total: 3,904 square feet

Width: 85'-5"
Depth: 74'-8"

The stone facade of this traditional design evokes images of a quieter life, a life of harmony and comfortable luxury. An elegant floor plan allows you to carry that feeling inside. The tiled foyer offers entry to any room you choose, whether it be the secluded den with its built-in bookshelves, the formal dining room, the formal living room with its fireplace, wet bar and wall of windows, or the spacious rear family and kitchen area with its sunny breakfast nook. The master suite offers privacy on the first floor and features a sitting room with bookshelves, two walk-in closets and a private bath with a corner whirlpool tub. Three family bedrooms, each with a walk-in closet, and two baths make up the second floor.

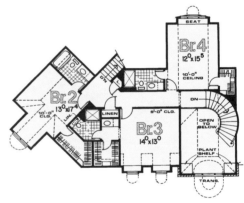

DESIGN HPT800015

First Floor: 2,617 square feet
Second Floor: 1,072 square feet
Total: 3,689 square feet

Width: 83'-5"
Depth: 73'-4"

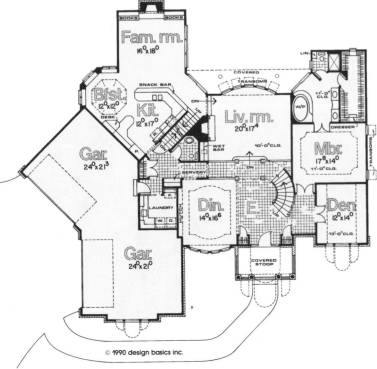

© 1990 design basics inc.

A spectacular volume entry with a curving staircase opens through columns to the formal areas of this home. The sunken living room contains a fireplace, a wet bar and a bowed window overlooking the back property, while the front-facing dining room offers a built-in hutch and a handy servery. The family room, with bookcases surrounding a fireplace, is open to a bayed breakfast nook, and both are easily served from the nearby kitchen. Placed away from the living area of the home, the den provides a quiet retreat and a stunning window. The master suite on the first floor contains a most elegant bath and a huge walk-in closet. Second-floor bedrooms also include walk-in closets and private baths.

First Floor: 3,218 square feet
Second Floor: 1,240 square feet
Total: 4,458 square feet

Bonus Room: 656 square feet
Width: 76'-0"
Depth: 73'-10"

This design features a breathtaking elevation all around, with an upper rear balcony, four covered porches and an inconspicuous side garage. The foyer is flanked by the dining room and the two-story library, which includes a fireplace and built-in bookcases. The elegant master bath provides dual vanities, a bright radius window and a separate leaded-glass shower. A unique double-decker walk-in closet provides plenty of storage. Nearby, a home office offers stunning views of the backyard. Upstairs, two family bedrooms share a compartmented bath and a covered porch, while a third bedroom offers a private bath. A bonus room is included for future expansion.

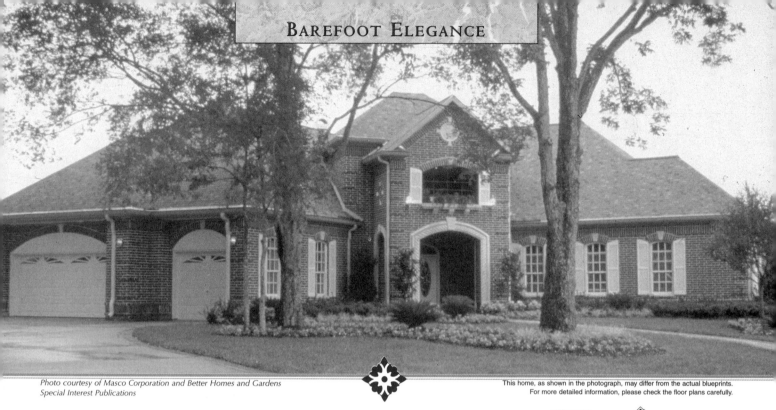

BAREFOOT ELEGANCE

Photo courtesy of Masco Corporation and Better Homes and Gardens Special Interest Publications

This home, as shown in the photograph, may differ from the actual blueprints. For more detailed information, please check the floor plans carefully.

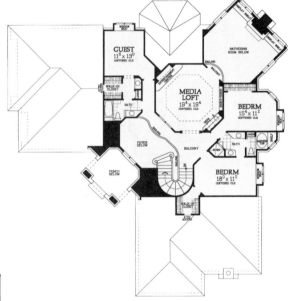

DESIGN HPT800017

First Floor: 3,297 square feet

Second Floor: 1,453 square feet

Total: 4,750 square feet

Width: 80'-10"
Depth: 85'-6"

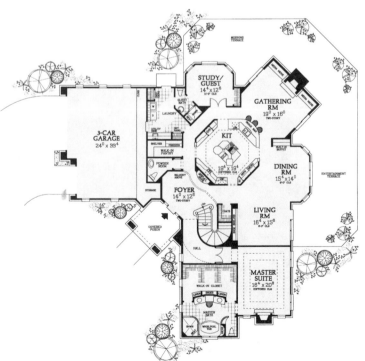

This elegant home combines a traditional exterior with a contemporary interior and provides a delightful setting for both entertaining and individual solitude. A living room and bay-windowed dining room provide an open area for formal entertaining, which can spill outside to the entertainment terrace or to the nearby gathering room with its dramatic fireplace. On the opposite side of the house, French doors make it possible for the study/guest room to be closed off from the rest of the first floor. The master suite is also a private retreat, offering a fireplace as well as an abundance of natural light, and a bath designed to pamper. The entire family will enjoy the second-floor media loft from which a balcony overlooks the two-story gathering room below.

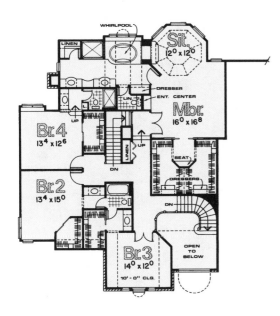

Second floor labels: WHIRLPOOL, LINEN, Sit. 12⁰ x 12⁰, DRESSER, ENT. CENTER, LIN., UP, Mbr. 16⁰ x 16⁸, Br. 4 13⁴ x 12⁶, LINEN, UP, SEAT, Br. 2 13⁴ x 15⁰, DN, DRESSERS, DN, Br. 3 14⁰ x 12⁰ 10'-0" CLG., OPEN TO BELOW

First Floor: 1,923 square feet
Second Floor: 1,852 square feet
Total: 3,775 square feet

Width: 70'-0"
Depth: 60'-0"

Breathtaking details and bright windows highlight this luxurious two-story home. Just off the spectacular entry is an impressive private den. The curved hall between the living and dining rooms offers many formal entertaining options. In the family room, three arched windows, a built-in entertainment center and a fireplace flanked by bookcases enhance daily comfort. After ascending the front staircase and overlooking the dramatic entry, four large bedrooms are presented. Three secondary bedrooms have generous closet space and private access to a bath. A sumptuous master suite awaits the homeowners with its built-in entertainment center and His and Hers walk-in closets.

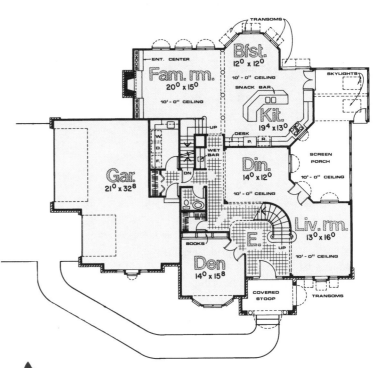

First floor labels: TRANSOMS, ENT. CENTER, Fam. rm. 20⁰ x 15⁰ 10'-0" CEILING, Bfst. 12⁰ x 12⁰ 10'-0" CEILING, SKYLIGHTS, SNACK BAR, Kit. 19⁴ x 13⁰, DESK, UP, Gar. 21⁰ x 32⁸, WET BAR, Din. 14⁰ x 12⁰ 10'-0" CEILING, SCREEN PORCH 10'-0" CEILING, DN, Liv. rm. 13⁰ x 16⁰ 10'-0" CEILING, BOOKS, E., UP, Den 14⁰ x 15⁸, COVERED STOOP, TRANSOMS

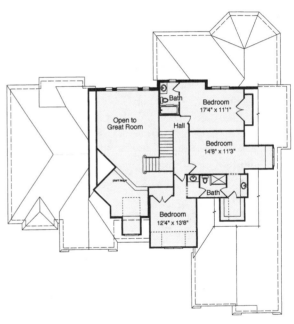

A combination of stone, brick, cedar shakes and arch-top windows creates the spectacular appearance of this stylish two-story home. Formal and informal spaces provide for various social events and comfortable family living. A gourmet kitchen with an open bar and island serves the dining room and breakfast area with equal ease. Sliding doors at the breakfast room provide access to a delightful rear porch, and multiple windows in the hearth room offer a favorable indoor-outdoor relationship. A secluded hall creates an orderly transition from the kitchen to the laundry and three-car garage. A wonderful master bedroom suite is decorated by a stepped ceiling, crown molding and a boxed window. Dual walk-in closets and a lavish dressing area with a platform whirlpool tub pamper the homeowner with luxury. Angled stairs with an open rail lead to a second-floor balcony and three additional bedrooms, each with large closets and private access to a bath.

DESIGN HPT800019

First Floor: 2,702 square feet
Second Floor: 986 square feet
Total: 3,688 square feet

Width: 75'-0"
Depth: 64'-11"

Covered Porch
16' x 13'6"

Bedroom
15'4" x 14'2"

Breakfast
14'5" x 14'9"

Hearth Room
14'10" x 15'4"

Master Bedroom
10' ceiling height
15' x 18'4"

Bath

Great Room
16' ceiling height
21' x 22

Kitchen
14'6" x 27'5"

Three Car Garage
23'6" x 39'2"

Hall

Dressing

Bath

Dining Room
13' ceiling height
14' x 17'6"

Foyer
13' ceiling height

Library
10' ceiling height
14'6" x 16'4"

Bath

Mud Room

Laun.

Porch

Unexcavated

Bedroom
14' x 13'0"

Mech.
15'4" x 10'6"

Bar
13'8" x 12'6"

Game Room
15' x 18'9"

Bath

Hall

Midia Room
36'9" x 22'8"

Billiards
21'2" x 16'6"

Unexcavated

Bath

Excercise Room
14' 13'10"

Unfinished Basement

Bedroom
14'8" x 16'4"

Unexcavated

Design HPT800020

Square Footage: 4,007
Finished Basement: 2,816 square feet
Width: 92'-0"
Depth: 76'-4"

This brick and stone combination lends a feeling of strength and stability to this home, a great foundation for any family. Corner quoins and classical columns decorate the exterior. Columns also play a decorative role inside as they separate the dining and great rooms from the foyer. The expansive great room features a grand fireplace and plenty of entertaining room. Open living area can be found in the hearth room—which also features a fireplace—breakfast room and spacious kitchen. The master bedroom includes huge walk-in closets, loft ceilings, and plenty of space in the dressing area. A family bedroom and library are also found on the first floor, while a game room—complete with billiards—media room, bar, exercise room and two more family bedrooms are found on the lower level.

DESIGN HPT800021

First Floor: 3,620 square feet
Second Floor: 2,440 square feet
Total: 6,060 square feet

Width: 139'-6"
Depth: 91'-1"

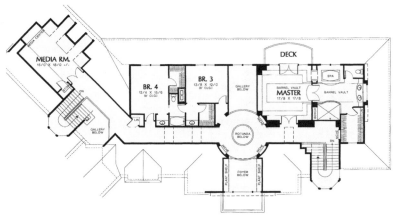

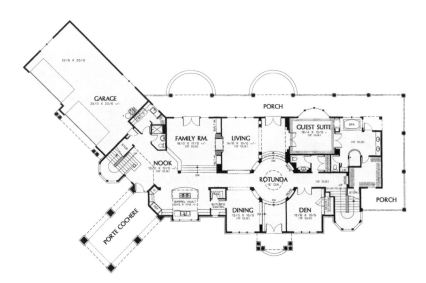

If it's space you desire, with a classy facade to further enhance it, this is the home for you! Inside, the foyer is flanked by a cozy den to the right and a formal dining room to the left. A lavish guest suite is loaded with amenities and is near the formal living room. The spacious kitchen will please any gourmet, with a cooktop island, walk-in pantry and a nearby sunken family room. Here, a fireplace, shared by the formal living room, will add warmth and charm to any gathering. Upstairs, two large bedrooms—each with walk-in closets and private lavatories—share a bath. A media room is just down the hall and is great for reading, studying or watching movies. The sumptuous master suite is designed to pamper, with such amenities as a walk-in closet, private deck, huge shower and separate spa tub. Note the tremendous amount of storage in the four-car garage.

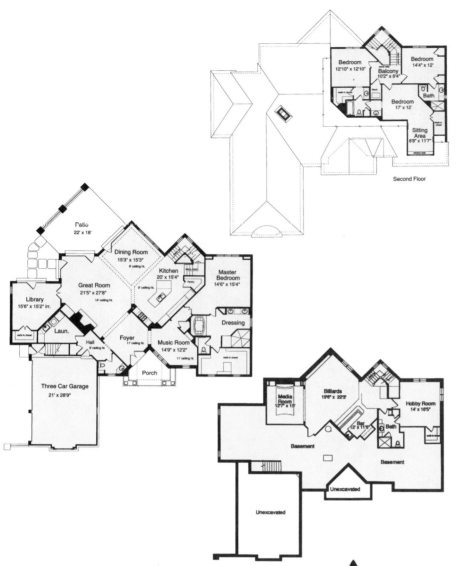

Second Floor

Bedroom 12'10" x 12'10"

Bedroom 14'4" x 12'

Balcony 10'2" x 6'4"

Bath

Bedroom 17' x 12'

Sitting Area 8'8" x 11'7"

Patio 22' x 18'

Dining Room 15'3" x 15'3"
9' ceiling ht.

Kitchen 20' x 15'4"
9' ceiling ht.

Master Bedroom 14'6" x 15'4"

Great Room 21'5" x 27'8"
14' ceiling ht.

Library 15'6" x 15'2" irr.

Laun.

Dressing

Hall

Foyer 11' ceiling ht.

Music Room 14'9" x 12'2"
11' ceiling ht.

Porch

Three Car Garage 21' x 28'9"

Media Room 12'7" x 15'

Billiards 19'6" x 22'3"

Hobby Room 14' x 16'5"

Bar 12' x 11'6"

Bath

Basement

Basement

Unexcavated

Unexcavated

DESIGN HPT800022

First Floor: 2,782 square feet
Second Floor: 1,027 square feet
Total: 3,809 square feet
Finished Basement: 1,316 square feet
Width: 78'-2"
Depth: 74'-6"

Filled with specialty rooms and abundant amenities, this country-side house is the perfect dream home. Double doors open into an angled foyer, flanked by a music room and a formal great room warmed by a fireplace. The music room leads to the master wing of the home, which includes a spacious bath with a dressing area and double walk-in closet. The great room is the heart of the home—being central with access to the island kitchen, formal dining room and library. Stairs behind the kitchen lead upstairs to a balcony, accessing three family bedrooms—one with a spacious sitting area. The lower level features a billiard room, hobby room, media room and future possibilities.

DESIGN HPT800023

First Floor: 3,414 square feet

Second Floor: 1,238 square feet

Total: 4,652 square feet

Width: 90'-6"
Depth: 78'-9"

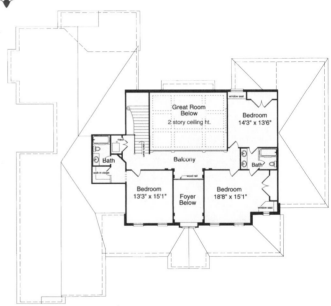

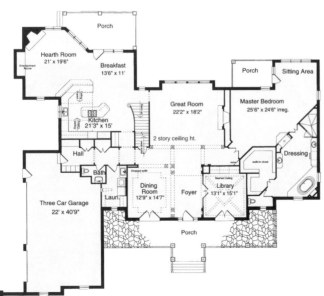

Country meets traditional in this splendid design. A covered front porch offers a place to enjoy the sunrise or place a porch swing. Gables, brick, stone and dormers bring out a comfortable appeal. With the formal areas flanking the foyer, an open flow is established between the column-accented dining room and the library with its distinguished beam ceiling. The two-story great room features a wall of windows looking out to the rear grounds. On the left, the gourmet kitchen serves up casual and formal meals to the breakfast and hearth rooms with the dining room just steps away. The master bedroom enjoys a sitting area with an array of view-catching windows, a spacious dressing area and an accommodating walk-in closet. Three family bedrooms—one with a private bath—complete the second level.

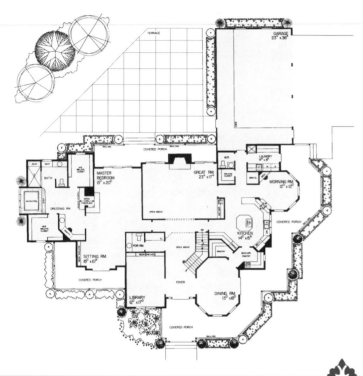

DESIGN HPT800024

First Floor: 2,995 square feet
Second Floor: 1,831 square feet
Total: 4,826 square feet

Width: 95'-0"
Depth: 99'-3"

A magnificent, finely wrought covered porch wraps around this impressive Victorian estate home. The two-story foyer provides a direct view past the stylish banister and into the great room with a large central fireplace. To the left of the foyer is a bookshelf-lined library and to the right is an octagonal dining room. The island cooktop serves as a convenient work space in the kitchen, and a pass-through connects this room with the morning room. A butler's pantry, walk-in closet and broom closet offer plenty of storage space. A luxurious master suite on the first floor opens to the rear covered porch. A through-fireplace warms the bedroom, sitting room and dressing room, which includes His and Hers walk-in closets. Four uniquely designed bedrooms, three full baths and a lounge with a fireplace are located on the second floor.

DESIGN HPT800025

First Floor: 3,739 square feet

Second Floor: 778 square feet

Total: 4,517 square feet

Width: 105'-0"
Depth: 84'-0"

The south of France, grand country flair, balconies and octagonal towers—this estate embraces the style of an elegant region. Double doors open to a formal columned foyer and give views of the octagonal living room beyond. To the left is the formal dining room that connects to the kitchen via a butler's pantry. To the right is an unusual den with octagonal reading space. The master wing is immense. It features a wet bar, private garden and exercise area. Two secondary bedrooms have private baths; Bedroom 2 has a private terrace. An additional bedroom with a private bath is on the second floor, making it a perfect student's retreat. Also on the second floor is a game loft and storage area.

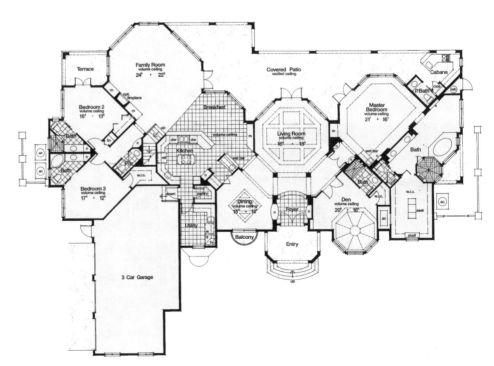

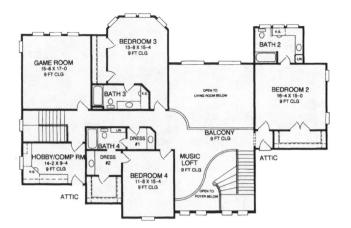

Second floor plan:
- **GAME ROOM** 15-6 X 17-0, 9 FT CLG
- **BEDROOM 3** 13-6 X 15-4, 9 FT CLG
- **BATH 2**
- **BATH 3**
- **BEDROOM 2** 16-4 X 15-0, 9 FT CLG
- **OPEN TO LIVING ROOM BELOW**
- **HOBBY/COMP RM** 14-2 X 9-4, 9 FT CLG
- **BATH 4**
- **DRESS #1**
- **DRESS #2**
- **BALCONY** 9 FT CLG
- **MUSIC LOFT** 9 FT CLG
- **BEDROOM 4** 11-8 X 15-4, 9 FT CLG
- **ATTIC**
- **OPEN TO FOYER BELOW**

First floor plan:
- **BRKFST ROOM** 13-6 X 10-6, 10 FT CLG
- **PORCH**
- **SITTING** 11-0 X 8-6, 10 FT CLG
- **FAMILY ROOM** 19-4 X 17-0, 10 FT CLG
- **FP**
- **KITCHEN** 13-6 X 15-0, 10 FT CLG
- **LIVING ROOM** 19-4 X 15-4, 2 STORY CLG
- **MASTER BEDROOM** 16-4 X 15-4, 10 FT CLG
- **PANTRY**
- **10 FT CLG**
- **UTIL** 12-4 X 9-6, 10 FT CLG
- **PWDR**
- **DINING ROOM** 14-0 X 16-0, 10 FT TRAY CLG
- **FOYER**
- **MASTER BATH** 10 FT CLG
- **2 STORY CLG**
- **PORCH**
- **RAISED STUDY** 13-6 X 13-6, 12 FT CLG
- **3 CAR GARAGE**

DESIGN HPT800026

First Floor: 3,058 square feet
Second Floor: 2,076 square feet
Total: 5,134 square feet

Width: 79'-6"
Depth: 73'-10"

This sweeping European facade, featuring a majestic turret-style bay, will easily be a neighborhood and family favorite. The foyer opens to a spacious formal area. Double doors from the living room open onto the rear porch. The master wing features a sitting area, luxurious master bath and two walk-in closets. The island kitchen opens to the bayed breakfast room. The family room offers a warm and relaxing fireplace. A study, three-car garage and utility room complete the first floor. Upstairs, three additional family bedrooms share the second floor with a music loft, hobby room and game room. Please specify basement, crawlspace or slab foundation when ordering.

BAREFOOT ELEGANCE

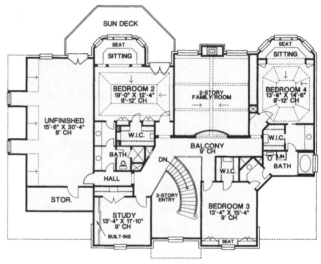

DESIGN HPT800027

First Floor: 2,595 square feet

Second Floor: 1,652 square feet

Total: 4,247 square feet

Width: 74'-11"
Depth: 60'-3"

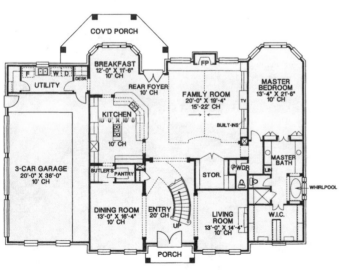

Dressed in white-as-lace snowfall, red orange fall leaves, or the greens and pastels of spring and summer, this home is handsome in all seasons. Its pediment and porch detailing enrich a facade ripe with traditional elements. Indulgent features are prominent on both floors. Grand bedrooms with sitting areas are great for homeowners and guests alike. The abundant storage space is fantastic for a growing or grown family. The formal and informal living areas make this home a dream for all who enter, whether it be close family or distant friends. A study on the second floor is a handy student's reading room. Unfinished bonus space can be completed later for a hobby room, game room or additional bedroom. Please specify basement or slab foundation when ordering.

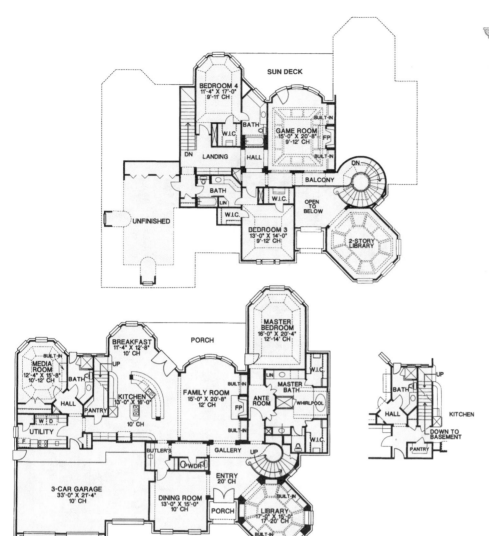

Second Floor (upper plan):

- SUN DECK
- BEDROOM 4 11'-4" X 17'-0" 9'-11" CH
- BATH
- W.I.C.
- DN
- LANDING
- HALL
- GAME ROOM 15'-0" X 20'-8" 9'-12" CH
- BUILT-IN
- FP
- BUILT-IN
- BATH
- LIN
- W.I.C.
- BALCONY
- DN
- UNFINISHED
- W.I.C.
- BEDROOM 3 13'-0" X 14'-0" 9'-12" CH
- OPEN TO BELOW
- 2-STORY LIBRARY

First Floor (lower plan):

- BUILT-IN
- MEDIA ROOM 12'-4" X 15'-8" 10'-12" CH
- BREAKFAST 11'-4" X 12'-8" 10' CH
- PORCH
- MASTER BEDROOM 16'-0" X 20'-4" 12'-14' CH
- BATH
- HALL
- KITCHEN 13'-0" X 16'-0"
- UP
- PANTRY
- FAMILY ROOM 15'-0" X 20'-8" 12' CH
- BUILT-IN
- LIN
- W.I.C.
- MASTER BATH
- WHIRLPOOL
- W/D
- UTILITY
- 10' CH
- FP
- ANTE ROOM
- BUILT-IN
- BUILT-IN
- W.I.C.
- 3-CAR GARAGE 33'-0" X 21'-4" 10' CH
- BUTLER'S
- WDR
- GALLERY
- UP
- DINING ROOM 13'-0" X 15'-0" 10' CH
- ENTRY 20' CH
- PORCH
- BUILT-IN
- LIBRARY 17'-0" X 15'-0" 17'-20' CH
- BUILT-IN
- PORTE-COCHERE

Alternate (small plan):

- UP
- BATH
- HALL
- KITCHEN
- DOWN TO BASEMENT
- PANTRY

DESIGN HPT800028

First Floor: 2,932 square feet
Second Floor: 1,407 square feet
Total: 4,339 square feet

Width: 80'-7"
Depth: 69'-7"

Celebrate independent spirit tempered with classical design. Keystone arches, full two-story windows and soaring rooflines marry with brick detailing and a porte cochere to proclaim grand styling. Not one amenity has been left out of the thoughtful floor plan, from built-in bookcases in the library to anteroom privacy in the master suite. The media room is hidden behind the three-car garage and makes a fine guest suite or maid's quarters. A game room on the second floor leads to a sun deck overlooking the backyard. Family bedrooms have private baths and walk-in closets. Please specify basement or slab foundation when ordering.

BAREFOOT ELEGANCE

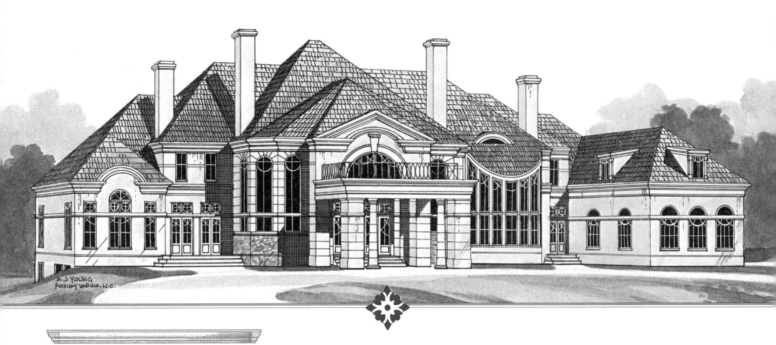

DESIGN HPT800029

First Floor: 4,351 square feet

Second Floor: 3,534 square feet

Total: 7,885 square feet

Bonus Space: 780 square feet

Width: 132'-0"

Depth: 75'-0"

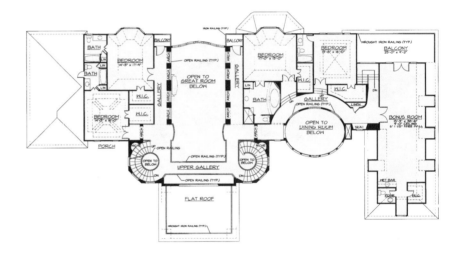

Y ou can almost hear the horses' hooves trotting along as they draw up to the porte cochere, depositing party-goers to the delights of this fine European estate. Resembling an historic estate home in France, this version was adapted to make even the fussiest homeowner of the modern-day world comfortable. The entry hall and grand hall are melded into one huge reception area, waiting for arriving guests. Serve formal dinners in the oval dining room with glass surrounding one whole side. The keeping room boasts a more casual atmosphere, but is decorated with a dazzling tray ceiling as accent. A gallery leads to the master suite, which also offers a tray ceiling, plus private access to a rear veranda. The master bath is a pampering haven, and provides access to a lavish walk-in closet. The second floor holds four secondary bedroom suites and an enormous bonus room to develop as needs arise. Don't miss the four-car garage at the right side of the plan.

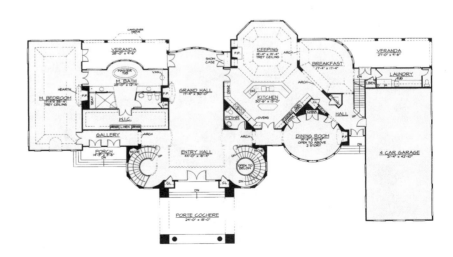

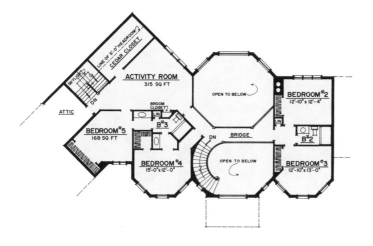

DESIGN HPT800030

First Floor: 2,960 square feet

Second Floor: 1,729 square feet

Total: 4,689 square feet

Width: 117'-4"
Depth: 59'-3"

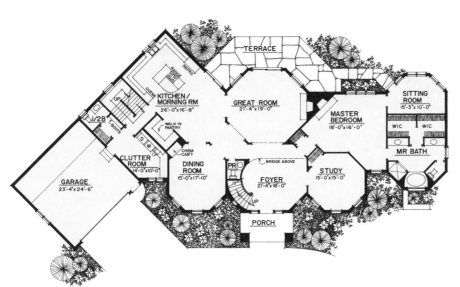

This stucco-and-stone chateau offers five bedrooms and a second-floor activity room within a European facade. Two front towers hold the formal dining room and a study on the first floor and two family bedrooms on the second floor. The great room is at the back of the plan and features a cozy hearth and sliding doors to the rear terrace. The master bedroom is also hearth-warmed and is graced by a sitting room and a bath with two walk-in closets. Casual gatherings occur in the kitchen/morning room, which features an island work center. Four family bedrooms inhabit the second floor and share two full baths.

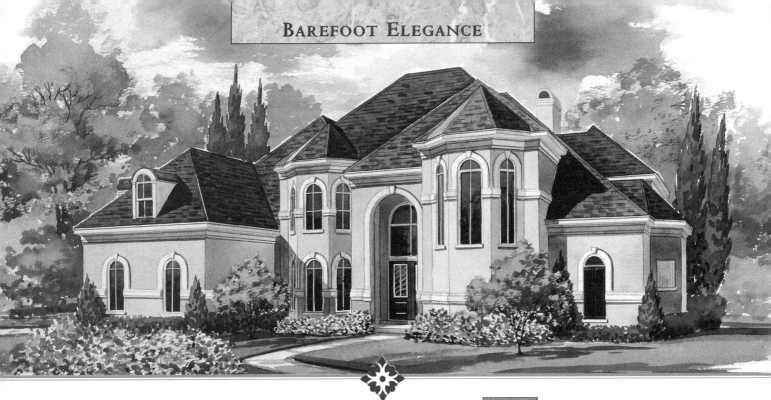

BAREFOOT ELEGANCE

DESIGN HPT800031

First Floor: 2,489 square feet

Second Floor: 1,650 square feet

Total: 4,139 square feet

Bonus Space: 378 square feet

Width: 72'-8"

Depth: 77'-0"

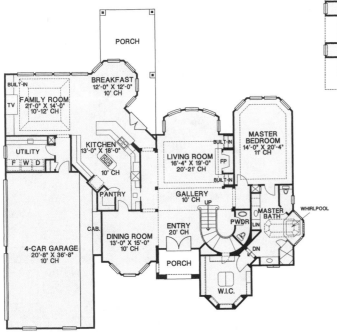

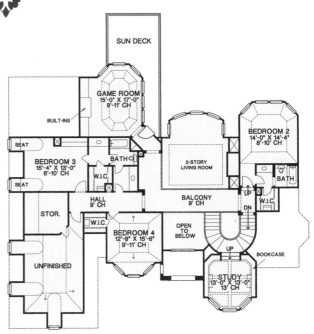

French and Mediterranean influences intermingle to bring their best points to this engaging residence. Details to be proud of include the double front entry, gallery hall, two-story living room and four bedrooms with stunning window accents. A dining porch, reached from the breakfast room, is covered by the sun deck on the second floor. A family room, nestled behind the four-car garage, features a tray ceiling and built-ins to host the entertainment center. The breakfast room and kitchen are nearby for casual dining. A game room on the second floor has a tray ceiling and built-ins. Please specify basement or slab foundation when ordering.

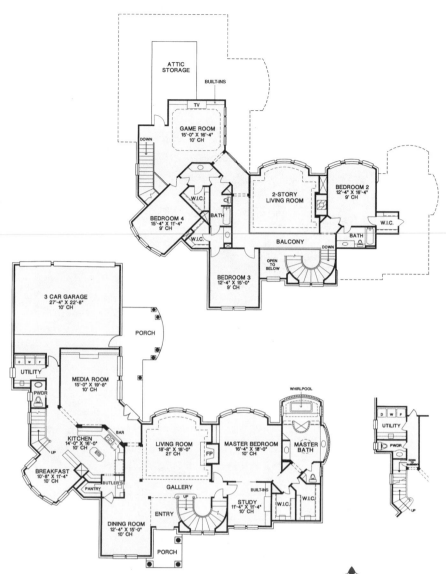

ATTIC
STORAGE

BUILT-INS

TV

GAME ROOM
15'-0" X 16'-4"
10' CH

DOWN

W.I.C.

BEDROOM 4
15'-4" X 11'-4"
9' CH

BATH

W.I.C.

2-STORY
LIVING ROOM

BEDROOM 2
12'-4" X 16'-4"
9' CH

W.I.C.

BATH

BALCONY

DOWN

OPEN
TO
BELOW

BEDROOM 3
12'-4" X 15'-0"
9' CH

3 CAR GARAGE
27'-4" X 22'-8"
10' CH

PORCH

D W F

UTILITY

PWDR

MEDIA ROOM
15'-0" X 19'-8"
10' CH

BAR

WHIRLPOOL

D W F

UTILITY

PWDR

KITCHEN
14'-0" X 16'-0"
10' CH

UP

LIVING ROOM
18'-8" X 18'-0"
21' CH

FP

MASTER BEDROOM
16'-4" X 18'-0"
10' CH

MASTER
BATH

BREAKFAST
10'-8" X 11'-4"
10' CH

BUTLER'S

PANTRY

GALLERY

UP

BUILT-INS

ENTRY

STUDY
11'-4" X 11'-4"
10' CH

W.I.C.

W.I.C.

UP

DINING ROOM
12'-4" X 15'-0"
10' CH

PORCH

DESIGN HPT800032

First Floor: 2,688 square feet
Second Floor: 1,540 square feet
Total: 4,228 square feet

Width: 84'-3"
Depth: 80'-1"

Light fills the interior of this estate, unifying the gallery, living room and dining room into one glorious formal space. A media room features built-ins and a bar. Much more than a mere bedroom, the master suite includes a private water closet, a glass-block-surrounded whirlpool tub and lavatory and two walk-in closets. The game room upstairs is the exclusive kids' domain and has a built-in entertainment center and rear stairs to the kitchen for late-night snacks. For guests, Bedroom 2 has its own private bath and a walk-in closet. Please specify basement or slab foundation when ordering.

BAREFOOT ELEGANCE

DESIGN HPT800033

First Floor: 2,430 square feet
Second Floor: 2,050 square feet
Total: 4,480 square feet

Width: 65'-0"
Depth: 69'-0"

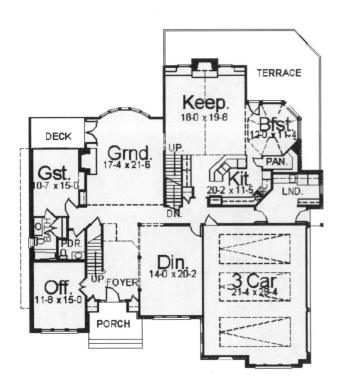

The fine brick exterior and Palladian windows lend a classic feel to this design, which speaks of modern-day comfort while recalling the past. A curved wall of glass is the highlight of the central grand room, which opens to a small side deck. A home office to the left of the foyer, accessed through double doors, provides convenience for busy family members. Fireplaces warm the grand room and keeping room, and the gourmet kitchen offers a large walk-in pantry. Family sleeping quarters reside upstairs—an expansive master suite with a private sitting area, walk-in closet and lavish bath fills the right wing, while three family bedrooms sit to the left.

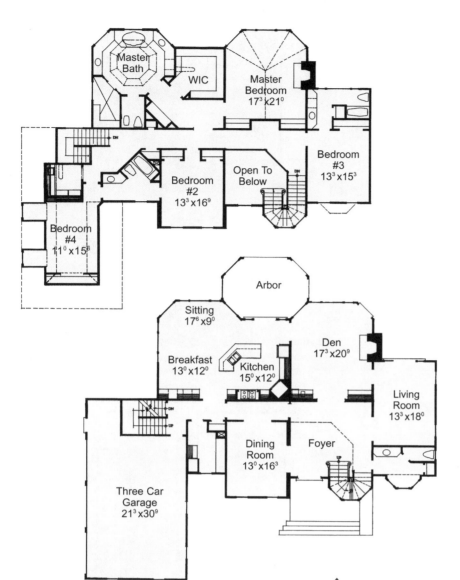

Master Bath

WIC

Master Bedroom
17³ x21⁰

Bedroom #2
13³ x16⁹

Open To Below

Bedroom #3
13³ x15³

Bedroom #4
11⁰ x15⁶

Arbor

Sitting
17⁶ x9⁰

Breakfast
13⁰ x12⁰

Kitchen
15⁰ x12⁰

Den
17³ x20⁹

Living Room
13³ x18⁰

Dining Room
13⁰ x16³

Foyer

Three Car Garage
21³ x30⁹

DESIGN HPT800034

First Floor: 2,161 square feet
Second Floor: 2,110 square feet
Total: 4,271 square feet

Width: 76'-2"
Depth: 60'-11"

A blend of stucco and stone creates the charm in this French Country estate home. The asymmetrical design and arched glass windows add to the European character. Inside, the plan offers a unique arrangement of rooms conducive to today's lifestyles. A living room and a dining room flank the foyer, creating a functional formal area. The large den or family room is positioned at the rear of the home with convenient access to the kitchen, patio and covered arbor. Equally accessible to the arbor and patio are the kitchen and breakfast/sitting area. A large butler's pantry is located near the kitchen and dining room. Upstairs, the vaulted master suite and three large bedrooms provide private retreats. This home is designed with a walkout basement foundation.

BAREFOOT ELEGANCE

DESIGN HPT800035

First Floor: 2,959 square feet

Second Floor: 1,326 square feet

Total: 4,285 square feet

Bonus Space: 999 square feet

Width: 90'-0"

Depth: 58'-8"

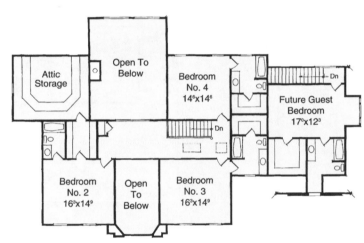

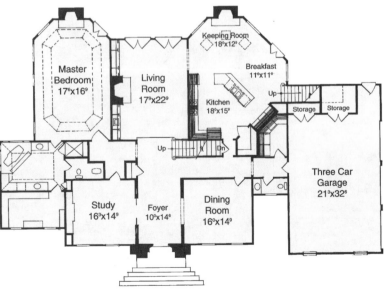

The impressive two-story facade with a raised front pediment gives this home a stately image. Inside, the two-story foyer opens to an adjacent study and dining room. An open rail from the gallery above looks down on the foyer and living room below to give a very open appeal to the formal area of the home. The master suite—with rich appointments and access to the study—provides the perfect retreat. The kitchen is situated in a casual arrangement with the breakfast area and keeping room. Upstairs, three large bedrooms and an optional guest suite, maid's quarters or bonus room meet the needs of a growing family. This home is designed with a walkout basement foundation.

DESIGN HPT800036

First Floor: 3,365 square feet
Second Floor: 1,456 square feet
Total: 4,821 square feet

Bonus Space: 341 square feet
Width: 81'-0"
Depth: 71'-9"

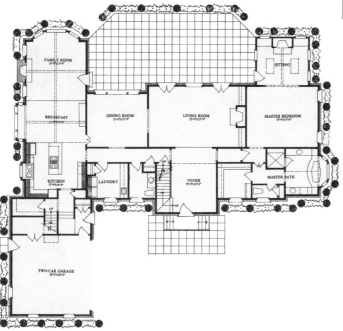

The graceful lines of this formal Georgian brick manor are an inviting presence in any neighborhood. An open foyer enjoys views of the back property through the living room, which features a fireplace framed with built-in bookshelves. Dinner guests will want to linger on the rear terrace, which opens through French doors from formal and casual areas. The gourmet kitchen has a cooktop island, a walk-in pantry and a breakfast area that's open to the bright family room. Homeowners will enjoy the master bedroom's private sitting area, which features two skylights, a fireplace and access to the terrace. This home is designed with a walk-out basement foundation.

DESIGN HPT800037

First Floor: 1,865 square feet

Second Floor: 1,694 square feet

Total: 3,559 square feet

Width: 59'-10"

Depth: 50'-0"

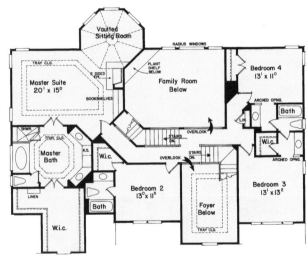

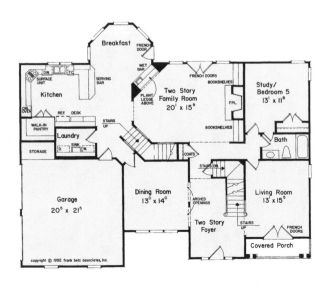

High ceilings and big windows combine to produce openness and light. Arched openings outline the entrance from the foyer to the formal dining room. The living room promises tranquility and privacy with its own covered porch. Additional work or entertainment space is provided by the quiet study/bedroom. The kitchen features a serving bar, built-in desk, walk-in pantry and plenty of counter space. Upstairs, the master suite includes a vaulted sitting room, linen storage, large walk-in closets and a compartmented bathroom with a garden tub. Three additional family bedrooms share two bathrooms and a balcony overlook to the family room below. Please specify basement or crawlspace foundation when ordering.

DESIGN HPT800038

First Floor: 1,786 square feet
Second Floor: 1,739 square feet
Total: 3,525 square feet

Width: 59'-0"
Depth: 53'-0"

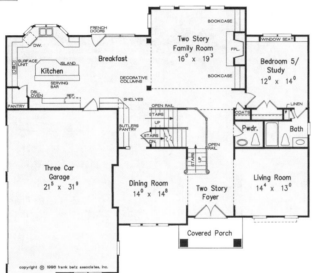

European details dress up this home that includes a two-story family room with a centered fireplace. Built-in bookcases and decorative columns are extra attractions in the family room. A butler's pantry eases serving in the dining room; nearby, the breakfast room offers French-door access to the rear property. Bedroom 5, secluded to the rear of the first floor, features a charming window seat, while the second floor contains a generous master suite and three family bedrooms—one with a private bath. Please specify basement or crawlspace foundation when ordering.

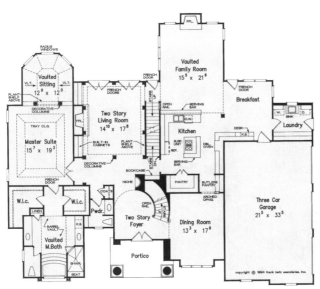

DESIGN HPT800039

First Floor: 2,764 square feet

Second Floor: 1,598 square feet

Total: 4,362 square feet

Width: 74'-6"
Depth: 65'-10"

Keystones and lintels wrap each window of this elegant facade in delicate decoration. Predominant pillars strengthen the aura of the entryway. Plenty of windows lend the home a bright, airy feel. The portico enters into a grand two-story foyer and extends to the two-story living room which features a hearth and two sets of French doors which open to the backyard. The vaulted family room also showcases a warming fireplace—perfect for rounding up the family and settling down for some quality family time. The master suite offers a sitting area, His and Hers walk-in closets and an extra-lush bath. Three family bedrooms are located on the second level.

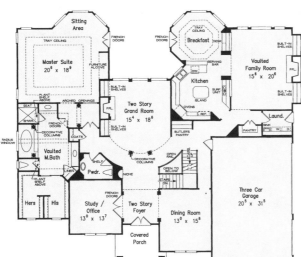

DESIGN HPT800040

First Floor: 3,085 square feet
Second Floor: 1,597 square feet
Total: 4,682 square feet

Width: 72'-4"
Depth: 65'-6"

The heart of this magnificent design is the two-story grand room with its coffered ceiling, fireplace flanked by built-in bookshelves and its wall of windows. The family living area on the right consists of a formal dining room, an island kitchen, a sunny breakfast nook with French-door access to the rear patio and a vaulted family room with a fireplace. The private master wing features a secluded office or study, a large master suite with a bayed sitting area, patio access and a vaulted bath with two walk-in closets, individual sinks and a separate tub and shower. Located upstairs are three family bedrooms, all with walk-in closets, and a large loft. Bedrooms 3 and 4 each include a built-in desk; Bedroom 2 features a private bath.

DESIGN HPT800041

First Floor: 3,926 square feet
Second Floor: 1,224 square feet
Total: 5,150 square feet

Width: 108'-0"
Depth: 89'-0"

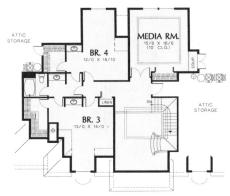

Corner quoins and rounded-top windows make an elegant statement on this luxury home. Through the double-door entrance, the foyer is flanked by the formal dining and living rooms to the left and an office to the right. The family room, defined by decorative columns, is straight ahead, and has a corner fireplace and a wet bar. The kitchen has a large cooktop island and a huge walk-in pantry and easily connects to the dining room through a convenient butler's pantry. The right side of the plan is given over to the master suite, including a compartmented bath with a garden tub and a room-sized walk-in closet. A guest bedroom, with its own bath, and a laundry room round out the first floor. Two additional bedrooms share a bath upstairs, along with a large media room. There is also room for a workshop in the four-car garage.

DESIGN HPT800042

First Floor: 2,951 square feet
Second Floor: 1,805 square feet
Total: 4,756 square feet

Width: 84'-6"
Depth: 64'-10"

Elegant quoins and European styling will allow this home to fit into an established neighborhood or distinguish a new one. Inside, the library—with a fireplace—to the left and a dining room with bay window to the right are perfect for entertaining on formal occasions. The living room features a fireplace and three sets of French doors to the rear. A master suite enjoys seclusion and private French doors to the rear. The open kitchen features an island and has direct access to the family room. Three family bedrooms are located on the second level, each room with a private bath and walk-in closet. This home is designed with a walkout basement foundation.

DESIGN HPT800043

First Floor: 3,098 square feet

Second Floor: 1,113 square feet

Total: 4,211 square feet

Bonus Room: 567 square feet

Width: 112'-0"

Depth: 69'-9"

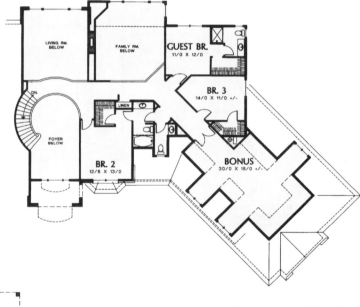

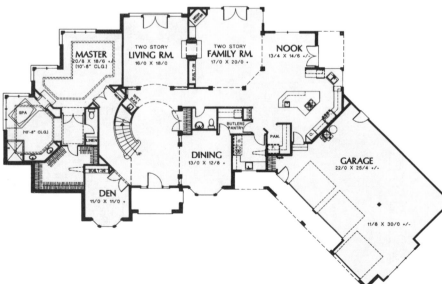

The magnificent entry of this elegant traditional home makes a grand impression. The soaring ceiling of the foyer looks over a curved staircase that leads to secondary sleeping quarters. The first-floor master suite offers an expansive retreat for the homeowner, with mitered windows and a see-through fireplace shared with the spacious, spa-style bath. Formal rooms open from the foyer, while a gallery hall leads to the casual living area, with a two-story family room and French doors to the outside. The three-car garage offers extra storage space. Two family bedrooms, one guest bedroom and a bonus room are found on the second level. Each bedroom benefits from individual baths.

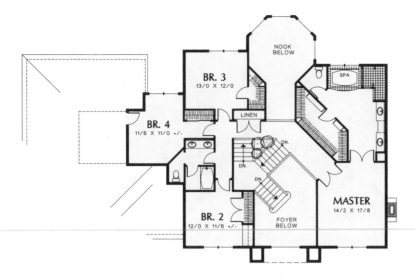

BR. 3
13/0 X 12/0

BR. 4
11/6 X 11/0 +/-

LINEN

SPA

DN.

DN.

DN.

MASTER
14/2 X 17/8

BR. 2
12/0 X 11/6 +/-

FOYER
BELOW

NOOK
BELOW

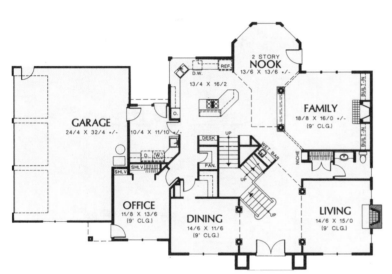

GARAGE
24/4 X 32/4 +/-

REF.

D.W.

2 STORY
NOOK
13/6 X 13/6 +/-
13/4 X 16/2

FAMILY
18/8 X 16/0 +/-
(9' CLG.)

BUILT-IN

BUILT-IN

DESK

UP

WET BAR

NICHE

10/4 X 11/10

SHLV.

SHLV.

D.

W.

PAN.

UP

UP

OFFICE
11/8 X 13/6
(9' CLG.)

DINING
14/6 X 11/6
(9' CLG.)

LIVING
14/6 X 15/0
(9' CLG.)

DESIGN HPT800044

First Floor: 2,150 square feet

Second Floor: 1,512 square feet

Total: 3,662 square feet

Width: 76'-0"
Depth: 52'-4"

Turn your dreams into a livable reality with this majestic European-style home. First impressions count even more when the entry foyer is as grand as this: two stories lit by clerestory windows, framed by the formal dining and living rooms and accented with column doorways. A dramatic, twin ascent staircase precedes the family room, made cozy with a fireplace and built-ins. Open to this casual, family living area is the gourmet kitchen and breathtaking, two-story breakfast nook. The kitchen is equipped with a cooktop island, considerable cabinet space, planning desk and a large butler's pantry to the dining room. A home office with a private outside entry completes the main floor. Upstairs, the impressive master suite features a huge walk-in closet and a spa-style bath. Three family bedrooms share a large hall bath.

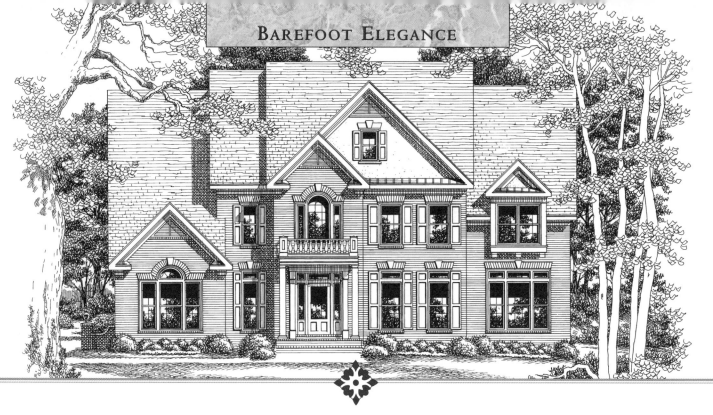

BAREFOOT ELEGANCE

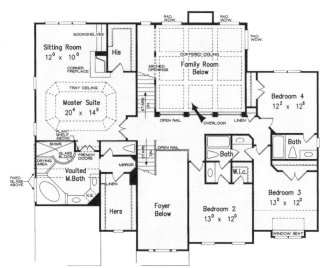

DESIGN HPT800179

First Floor: 1,854 square feet
Second Floor: 1,738 square feet
Total: 3,592 square feet

Width: 58'-0"
Depth: 52'-4"

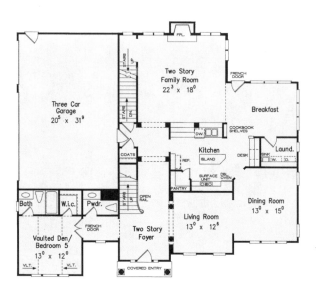

Gables, shutters and arched windows combine with fine brick detailing to give this home plenty of curb appeal. Inside, the two-story foyer is flanked by the formal living room and a hallway to the den (or make it a guest suite). The efficient kitchen offers an island and a walk-in pantry and has easy access to the formal dining room, sunny breakfast room and the two-story family room. Note the two sets of stairs to the second floor. Upstairs, three secondary bedrooms share two baths and an overlook into the family room. A deluxe master bedroom suite features a sitting room, corner fireplace, His and Hers walk-in closets and a lavish, vaulted bath. A three-car garage easily shelters the family fleet. Please specify basement or crawlspace foundation when ordering.

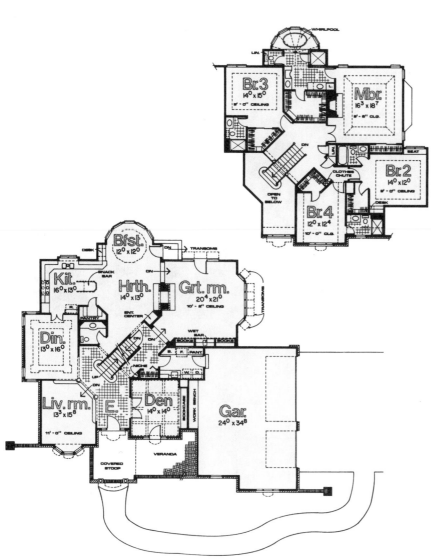

Design HPT800045

First Floor: 2,126 square feet
Second Floor: 1,680 square feet
Total: 3,806 square feet

Width: 67'-4"
Depth: 66'-0"

A striking elevation imparts an "Old World" image with repetitive peaks, elegant windows and a covered stoop framed by stately columns. The formal dining room with unique ceiling detail opens to a sunken living room. The living room then leads to the den, which offers a formal setting with French doors, a spider-beamed ceiling and a built-in bookcase. A fully equipped kitchen holds a large walk-in pantry and rounded breakfast area which is open to the hearth room. All the bedrooms enjoy special ceiling details, walk-in closets and private baths. The master suite features a fireplace and a luxurious bath with a glass-block shower and a two-person whirlpool tub surrounded by windows.

DESIGN HPT800046

First Floor: 2,771 square feet

Second Floor: 1,420 square feet

Total: 4,191 square feet

Width: 77'-8"

Depth: 68'-4"

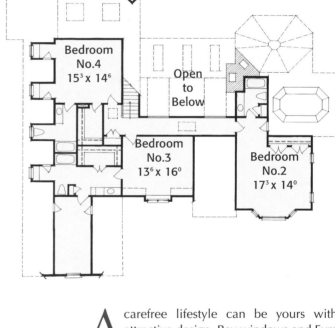

A carefree lifestyle can be yours with this attractive design. Bay windows and European accents decorate the exterior, while a variety of comfortable rooms fill the interior. Skylights enhance the living room and keeping room; fireplaces can be found in the living room, keeping room and master-suite sitting room. The cozy breakfast room, a perfect place for informal meals, features two full walls of windows. Sleeping quarters consist of an opulent first-floor master suite, with an expansive sitting area and a pampering bath, and three second-floor family bedrooms.

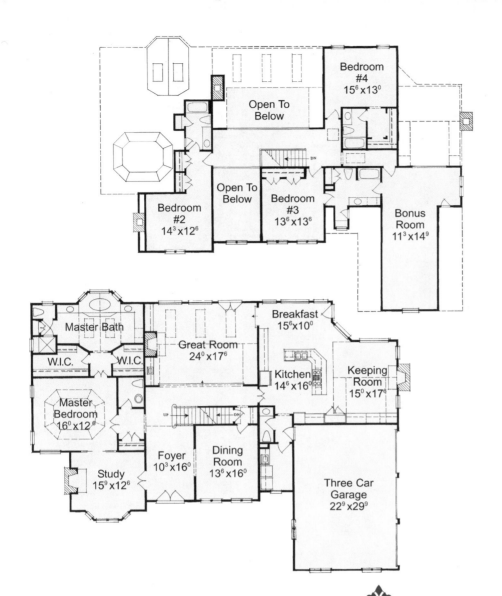

Second Floor:
Bedroom #4 15⁶ x 13⁰ → $15^6 \times 13^0$

Open To Below

Open To Below

Bedroom #2 14³ x 12⁶

Bedroom #3 13⁶ x 13⁶

Bonus Room 11³ x 14⁹

First Floor:
Master Bath

W.I.C. W.I.C.

Master Bedroom 16⁰ x 12⁶

Study 15⁹ x 12⁶

Great Room 24⁰ x 17⁶

Breakfast 15⁶ x 10⁰

Kitchen 14⁶ x 16⁰

Keeping Room 15⁰ x 17⁶

Foyer 10³ x 16⁰

Dining Room 13⁶ x 16⁰

Three Car Garage 22⁹ x 29⁹

DESIGN HPT800047

First Floor: 2,832 square feet
Second Floor: 1,394 square feet
Total: 4,226 square feet

Bonus Room: 425 square feet
Width: 81'-6"
Depth: 61'-6"

Inside this exquisite country estate, the arrangement of rooms is well-suited for a variety of lifestyles. The large dining room and great room provide the opportunity for formal receiving and entertaining. For casual living, look to the spacious kitchen, the multi-windowed breakfast room or the cozy keeping room with its welcoming fireplace. Conveniently yet privately located, the master suite is designed to take full advantage of the adjacent study and family area. The second floor contains three bedrooms, three full baths and a bonus room that also functions as Bedroom 5. This home is designed with a basement foundation.

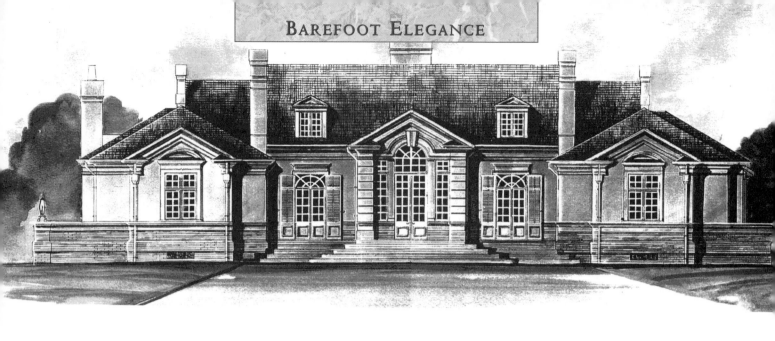

BAREFOOT ELEGANCE

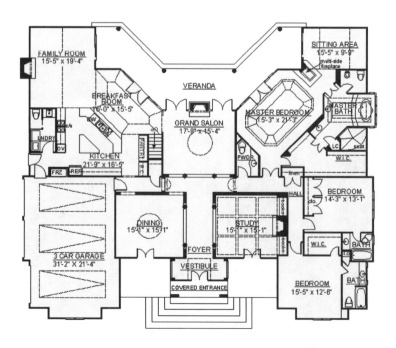

OFFICE
18'-1" x 15'-11"

clo.

attic access

BATH

down

attic access

CEDAR CLOSET

vlt. | vlt. | vlt.

PLAYROOM
23'-7" x 14'-1"

Design HPT800048

Square Footage: 3,823

Bonus Space: 1,018 square feet

Width: 80'-6"

Depth: 70'-8"

FAMILY ROOM
15'-5" x 19'-4"

SITTING AREA
15'-5" x 9'-9"
multi-side fireplace

BREAKFAST ROOM
16'-0" x 15'-5"

VERANDA

MASTER BEDROOM
15'-3" x 21'-3"

MASTER BATH

LNDRY

KITCHEN
21'-9" x 16'-5"

GRAND SALON
17'-9" x 45'-4"

PANTRY

LC seat

W.I.C.

FRZ | REF

PWDR.

linen

HALL

BEDROOM
14'-3" x 13'-1"

3 CAR GARAGE
31'-2" X 21'-4"

DINING
15'-1" x 15'-1"

STUDY
15'-1" x 15'-1"

FOYER

W.I.C.

BATH

VESTIBULE

COVERED ENTRANCE

BEDROOM
15'-5" x 12'-6"

BATH

This Neoclassical home has plenty to offer! The elegant entrance is flanked by a formal dining room on the left and a beam-ceilinged study—complete with a fireplace—on the right. An angled kitchen is sure to please with a work island, plenty of counter and cabinet space, and a snack counter that it shares with the sunny breakfast room. A family room with a second fireplace is nearby. The lavish master suite features many amenities, including a huge walk-in closet, a three-sided fireplace and a lavish bath. Two secondary bedrooms have private baths. Finish the second-floor bonus space to create an office, a playroom and a full bath. A three-car garage easily shelters the family fleet.

On the Waterfront

Elegant estates suitable for resort lifestyles

Design HPT800050, see page 81

DESIGN HPT800049

First Floor: 2,491 square feet

Second Floor: 1,290 square feet

Total: 3,781 square feet

Finished Basement: 358 square feet

Width: 62'-0"

Depth: 67'-0"

A n engaging blend of comfort and high architectural style creates a high-spirited home that's worthy of attention and is downright inviting. The foyer provides a magnificent view through the great room, where a two-story glass wall allows the vista to extend to the rear property. Bedroom 4 shares a fireplace with the great room, while Bedroom 3 provides a beautiful bay window. The wraparound veranda includes an outdoor kitchen with a grill, rinsing sink and pass-through to the main kitchen. The upper-level master suite has its own observation deck and a socko bath with a fireplace, angled whirlpool tub, oversized shower, separate vanities and a walk-in closet with a dressing island. A gallery leads to an elevator and across the catwalk with an overlook to the great room. At the end of the hall, a spacious bedroom offers its own bath and deck, and enough wardrobe space for a live-in guest.

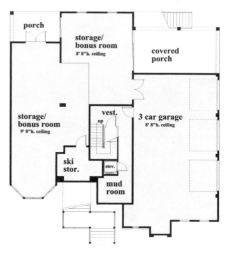

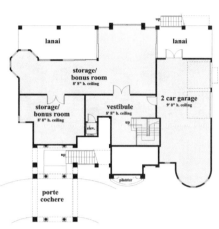

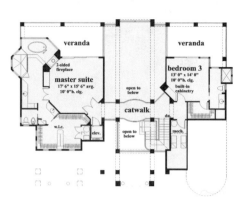

First floor plan labels: outdoor kitchen, veranda, nook, great room 20' 0" x 24' 0" 2-story clg., veranda, kitchen, dining 14' 0" x 11' 8" 10' 0" h. clg., built-in cabinetry, study 11' 10" x 14' 0" 10' 0" h. clg., pantry, server, wetbar, 2-sided fireplace, window seat, ut., p., elev., foyer, up, dn., w.l.c., bedrm 2 12' 0" x 16' 8" 14' 0" h. clg., entry, porte cochere

Basement plan labels: lanai, storage/bonus room 8' 8" h. ceiling, storage/bonus room 8' 8" h. ceiling, vestibule 8' 8" h. ceiling, lanai, 2 car garage 9' 0" h. ceiling, up, elev., up, up, planter, porte cochere

Second floor plan labels: veranda, veranda, 2-sided fireplace, master suite 17' 6" x 14' 0" 10' 0" h. clg., open to below, bedroom 3 13' 0" x 14' 0" 10' 0" h. clg., built-in cabinetry, w.i.c., elev., catwalk, open to below, dn., mech.

DESIGN HPT800050

First Floor: 2,391 square feet

Second Floor: 1,539 square feet

Total: 3,930 square feet

Finished Basement: 429 square feet
Width: 71'-0"
Depth: 69'-0"

Impressive pillars, keystone lintel arches, a covered carport, an abundance of windows and an alluring fountain are just a few of the decorative touches of this elegant design. The two-story foyer leads to a two-story great room, which enjoys built-in cabinetry, a two-sided fireplace and spectacular views to the rear property. To the left of the great room is the dining area, with a wet bar, island kitchen and nearby bayed breakfast nook. Bedroom 2 boasts a semi-circular wall of windows, a full bath and a walk-in closet. The second-floor master suite is filled with amenities, including a two-sided fireplace, large walk-in closet, garden tub overlooking a private veranda, separate shower and compartmented toilet. Bedroom 3 also accesses a private veranda, as well as its own full bath.

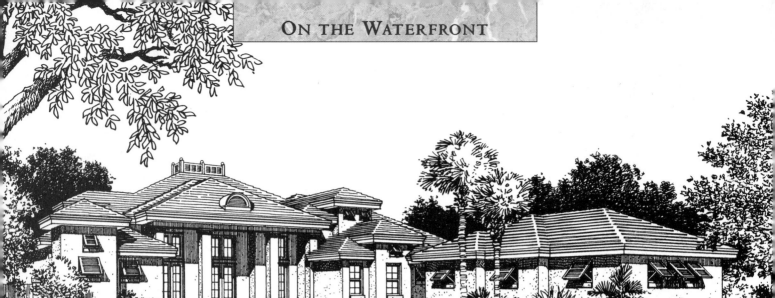

DESIGN HPT800051

Square Footage: 4,565
Bonus Room: 522 square feet
Width: 83'-8"
Depth: 89'-8"

Royalty on vacation—this is the promise of this chic British Carribean-style estate. A terra cotta veranda, with French doors topped with transoms, leads to a foyer flanked by a study and the formal dining room. The formal living room is framed by columns and lintels and has access to a covered patio surrounding the pool. The great room accesses another pool patio that features a handy summer kitchen. Sleeping areas are a delight. The master suite is separated from the family bedrooms and is entered through a foyer with a view of a private garden with a fountain. The master suite also has a sitting room, complete with a through-fireplace which can be viewed from the outdoor spa. A grandparents' suite allows space for visiting in-laws and has a small kitchenette for late-night snacks. Bonus space upstairs includes a full bath and would make a great game room/activity area.

This brick palace sits well on the waterfront— though elegant, it is also rugged. The facade of this home focuses on the powerful entry and steep rooflines. The foyer is flanked by the study and formal dining room. The lovely living room is angled in a special way that makes this home stand apart from the rest. Windows frame the living room and offer views of the covered lanai. The spacious kitchen has extra counter space and servability with the island facing both the leisure room and breakfast nook. The leisure room is ready for family time with a built-in entertainment center. A lavish master suite and convenient guest suite finish off the first floor. Two more guest suites, a loft and a covered observation deck make this seaside specialty all the more grand.

DESIGN HPT800052

First Floor: 3,010 square feet
Second Floor: 948 square feet
Total: 3,958 square feet

Width: 65'-0"
Depth: 91'-0"

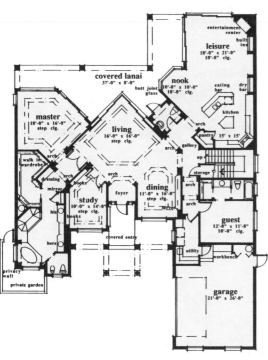

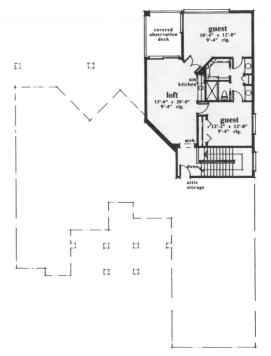

DESIGN HPT800053

First Floor: 2,618 square feet

Second Floor: 1,945 square feet

Total: 4,563 square feet

Width: 54'-8"
Depth: 97'-4"

Double doors open to a grand foyer with a formal dining room to the left. The nearby kitchen and nook combine with a multi-windowed two-story leisure room for more casual living, and an adjacent two-story living room for more formal pursuits. The first-floor master suite features a large walk-in closet, a luxurious bath and access to the rear veranda. The second floor contains a guest suite with a private bath and balcony, a bedroom/bonus room with its own balcony and a second master suite. This second master bedroom is highlighted by double doors opening onto a private deck. A walk-in closet, a spacious bath with a bumped-out tub and a separate shower provide finishing touches to this private suite.

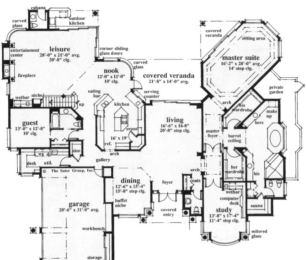

Design HPT800054

First Floor: 4,138 square feet
Second Floor: 1,269 square feet
Total: 5,407 square feet

Width: 90'-0"
Depth: 85'-0"

Elegant windows and columns define this gorgeous home. Light floods the interior with warmth and comfort. Most of the living in this grand home takes place on the first floor. A fireplace and built-in entertainment center are located in the leisure room, where a wet bar complements this room's function perfectly. This home is well-prepared for outdoor events with an outdoor kitchen and a serving counter, located just outside the leisure room through sliding doors—perfect for summertime parties. The indoor kitchen is well-lit by the covered glass breakfast nook—enjoy a quick snack at the eating bar. The relaxing living room showcases a wonderful view of the festivities taking place outdoors all year long. The lavish master suite features a private study, a marvelous bath and a bedroom with a stepped ceiling. Two guest suites are perfect for family and friends. A game loft and guest suite are located on the second floor.

DESIGN HPT800055

Square Footage: 3,506

Width: 85'-4"
Depth: 89'-4"

Does your family own a lot of cars? If so, this house is perfect for you. The master and family garages celebrate the passion for automobiles in a sensible way. The house itself breaks new design ground and addresses many concerns for the large family. A grand foyer leads to the invitingly large living room. Columns flank the formal dining room and help define the large nook across the hall. Family space abounds with a true informal dining room and a gourmet kitchen, which overlooks the glass-walled family room. The master wing is lavishly designed with a sitting room, private sleeping chamber and ultra-deluxe bath. Two large secondary bedrooms reside on the opposite side of the home and share a full bath that includes dual vanity sinks.

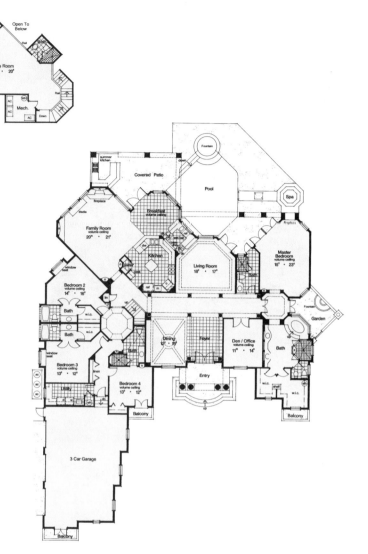

Open To Below

Bonus Room
24⁰ · 20⁰

Mech.

AC

AC

Down

DESIGN HPT800056

Square Footage: 4,222 square feet

Bonus Room: 590 square feet

Width: 83'-10"

Depth: 112'-0"

Fountain

summer kitchen

Covered Patio

Pool

Spa

fireplace

Media

Breakfast
volume ceiling

Family Room
volume ceiling
20⁰ · 21⁰

Kitchen

Living Room
18⁰ · 17⁰

Master Bedroom
volume ceiling
15⁰ · 23⁰

Bath

Bedroom 2
volume ceiling
14⁰ · 16⁰

Bath

w.i.c.

Bath

w.i.c.

Fountain

Garden

Dining
12⁰ · 15⁰

Foyer

Den / Office
volume ceiling
11⁰ · 14⁰

Bath

Bath

window seat

Bedroom 3
volume ceiling
13⁰ · 12⁰

linen

Bath

Bedroom 4
volume ceiling
13⁰ · 12⁰

Entry

w.i.c.

shelf

w.i.c.

Balcony

Balcony

3 Car Garage

Balcony

The striking facade of this magnificent estate is just the beginning of the excitement you will encounter inside. The entry foyer passes the formal dining room to the columned gallery, which leads to all regions of the house, with the formal living room at the head. The living room opens to the rear patio and the showpiece pool lying flush against the dramatic rear windows of the house. A sunken wet bar serves the living room and the pool via a swim-up bar. The contemporary kitchen has a work island and all the amenities for gourmet preparation. The family room will be a favorite for casual entertainment. The family sleeping wing begins with an octagonal vestibule and has three bedrooms with private baths. The master wing has a private garden and an opulent bath.

DESIGN HPT800057

First Floor: 3,667 square feet

Second Floor: 1,867 square feet

Total: 5,534 square feet

Bonus Room: 140 square feet

Width: 102'-0"

Depth: 87'-0"

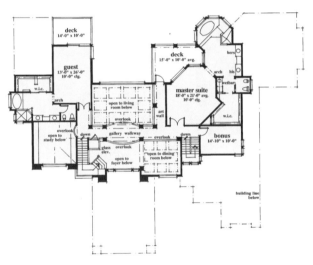

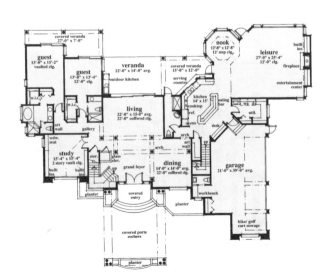

Sweeping heights lend a grand stroke to many of the rooms in this estate: the study, the grand foyer, the dining room and the living room. The living and dining room ceilings are also coffered. Upstairs, the master suite enjoys a full list of appointments, including an exercise (or bonus) room, a tub tower with a cove-lit ceiling and a private deck. Also on this floor is a guest bedroom with an observation deck (or make this a spectacular study to complement the master suite). Other special details: a pass-through outdoor bar, an outdoor kitchen, a workshop area, two verandas and a glass elevator.

Floor Plan Labels

built ins

guest
14'-4" x 14'-6"
tray clg.

books

entertainment center

leisure
25'-0" x 19'-10"
13'-4" flat clg.

fireplace

nook
11'-0" x 11'-0"
13'-4" flat clg.

lanai

outdoor kitchen

sitting

am kitchen

corner fireplace

master suite
17'-0" x 32'-0"
13'-4" flat clg.

curved glass

his

guest
12'-8" x 12'-4"
9'-4" flat clg.

kitchen
14'-0" x 18'-0"

living
15'-0" x 14'-0"
vaulted clg.

hers

sauna

utility

gallery

wetbar

exer.
10' x 14'

garage
22'-8" x 30'-8"

dining
11'-4" x 15'-0"
vaulted clg.

foyer

study
14'-1" x 20'-0"
13'-4" flat clg.

entry

curved glass

workbench

DESIGN HPT800058

Square Footage: 4,565

Width: 88'-0"
Depth: 95'-0"

A free-standing entryway is the focal point of this luxurious residence. It has an arch motif that is carried through to the rear using a gabled roof and a vaulted ceiling from the foyer out to the lanai. The kitchen, which features a cooktop island and plenty of counter space, opens to the leisure area with a handy snack bar. Two guest suites with private baths are just off this casual living area. The master wing is truly pampering, stretching the entire length of the home. The suite has a large sitting area, a corner fireplace and a morning kitchen. The bath features an island vanity, a raised tub with a curved glass wall overlooking a private garden, a sauna and separate closets. An exercise room has a curved glass wall and a pocket door to the study, where a wet bar is ready to serve up refreshment.

DESIGN HPT800059

First Floor: 4,284 square feet

Second Floor: 1,319 square feet

Total: 5,603 square feet

Width: 109'-4"
Depth: 73'-2"

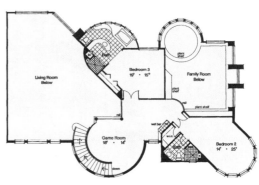

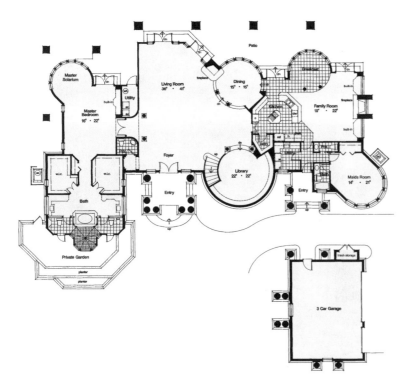

A hint of Moroccan architecture, with columns, arches and walls of glass, makes an arresting appearance in this home. It allows a diverse arrangement of space inside, for a dynamic floor plan. The foyer spills into the immense living area and sunken dining room. A stair encircles the sunken library—a great space for a home theater. Beyond is the family room with a two-story high media wall and built-ins, plus the circular breakfast room and island kitchen. A maid's room, or guest room, has a full circular wall of glass and leads to the garage through a covered entry and drive-through area. The master suite is true luxury: a circular sitting area, His and Hers facilities and a private garden. Upstairs is a game room, plus two family bedrooms with private amenity-filled baths.

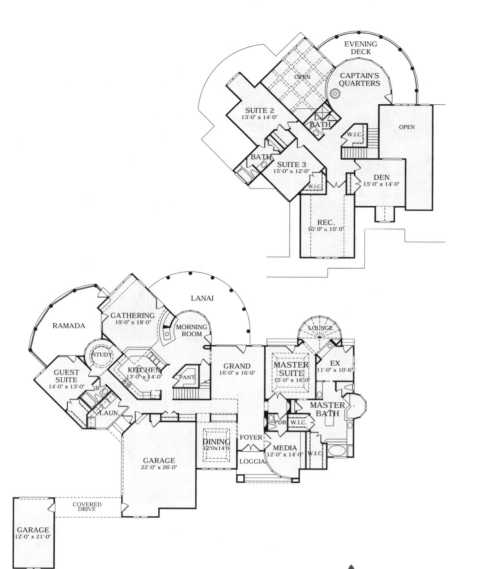

DESIGN HPT800060

First Floor: 3,329 square feet
Second Floor: 1,485 square feet
Total: 4,814 square feet

Width: 106'-6"
Depth: 89'-10"

From the elegant entrance with a curved wall of windows leading to the front door, to the wonderful angles used throughout the home, this is a plan sure to please. Study the master bedroom suite and you'll see that amenities haven't been neglected: two walk-in closets, a lavish bath with a separate tub and shower and two vanities, a separate unique lounge and an exercise room. On the other end of the home, find the highly efficient kitchen, a spacious gathering room, a round morning room and study and a quiet guest suite. The second level is equally deluxe with two suites, a recreation room, a quiet den and a large open area called the captain's quarters that opens to an evening deck.

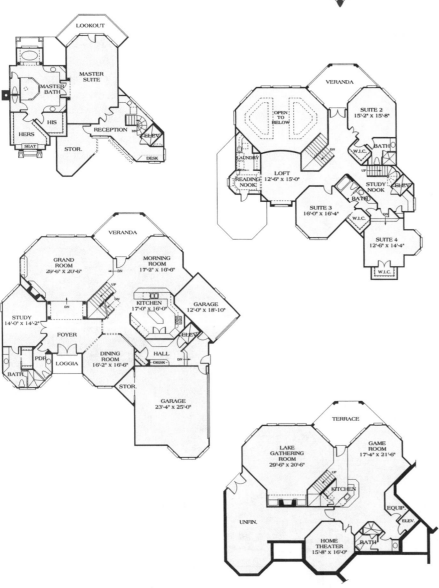

A level for everyone! This home is sure to please every member of the family. On the first floor, there's a study with a full bath, a formal dining room, a grand room with a fireplace, and a fabulous kitchen with an adjacent morning room. The second floor contains three suites—each with walk-in closets—two full baths, a loft and a reading nook near the laundry room. A lavish master suite on the third floor is full of amenities, including His and Hers walk-in closets, a huge private bath and a balcony. In the basement, casual entertaining takes off with a large gathering room, a home theater and a spacious game room.

DESIGN HPT800061

First Level: 2,347 square feet
Second Level: 1,800 square feet
Third Level: 1,182 square feet
Total: 5,329 square feet
Finished Basement: 1,688 square feet
Width: 75'-5"
Depth: 76'-4"

DESIGN HPT800062

First Floor: 2,425 square feet

Second Floor: 1,398 square feet

Total: 3,823 square feet

Finished Basement: 705 square feet

Bonus Space: 176 square feet

Width: 64'-10"

Depth: 66'-4"

This home is designed with a walkout basement, making it perfect for hillside locations. A veranda wraps the corners of this home on the first and second levels. Columns define the dining and living rooms—creating an elegantly formal entertaining area. A fireplace is located in the gathering room, where French doors open to the rear deck. The breakfast nook—which also accesses the rear deck—is closely connected to the snack-bar kitchen. French doors lead to the sun room from the kitchen and from the sun room to the front veranda. A lavish master suite is located on the first level. Three family suites make comfortable sleeping quarters on the second level.

DESIGN HPT800063

First Floor: 2,290 square feet

Second Floor: 2,142 square feet

Total: 4,432 square feet

Width: 95'-9"
Depth: 73'-0"

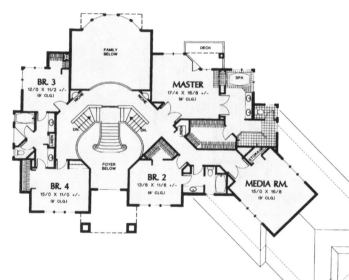

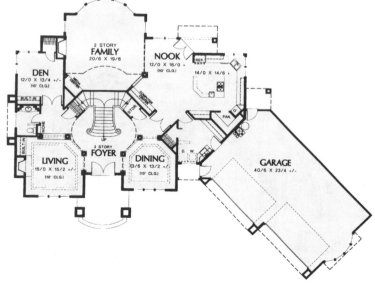

An impressive entry opens onto a two-story foyer with a magnificent staircase. Formal living comes to the forefront with a columned dining room on the right and an inviting living room to the left. The kitchen is a connoisseur's delight, complete with a large pantry and a nook that contains a computer center. The two-story family room is the center of attention with its unique wall of bow windows and a cheerful fireplace. A den and powder room complete the first floor. The second floor holds three secondary bedrooms, two full baths, a media room and an elegant master suite with a private deck and a deluxe master bath.

DESIGN HPT800064

Main Level: 2,274 square feet
Second Level: 1,380 square feet
Total: 3,654 square feet

Finished Basement: 1,906 square feet
Width: 72'-0"
Depth: 63'-0"

This multi-level contemporary home offers an array of winning combinations to make it truly unique and enjoyable. On the main level, the living and dining rooms are open to each other, creating ample space for entertaining and featuring a fireplace and a shared wet bar. The informal area combines a large family room, boasting another fireplace and outdoor access, with a sunny breakfast nook and an efficient kitchen. A secluded den and a powder room complete the main level. On the upper level, the master bedroom includes a separate sitting space, a spa bath and an immense walk-in closet. It shares space with a guest suite that could also be used as an office or study. On the lower level, two family bedrooms share a full bath and enjoy a game room (with a third fireplace) and a wine cellar.

DESIGN HPT800065

First Floor: 2,709 square feet

Second Floor: 2,321 square feet

Total: 5,030 square feet

Width: 121'-2"
Depth: 77'-7"

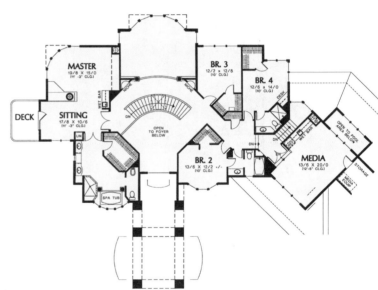

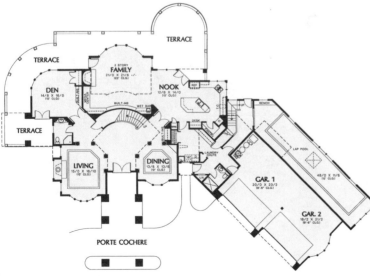

Grand columns define this superior home while soft windows add an elegant feel. A huge foyer with a curved staircase welcomes you to this palatial four-bedroom home. On the main floor, you'll find the dining room, living room, den, family room, kitchen and dining nook, laundry room, two powder rooms, the four-car garage and a lap pool. Terraces wrap partially around the home. On the second floor, the master suite includes a sitting room, deck, walk-in closet and compartmented bath. Three family bedrooms share two baths. The media room, also on the second floor, features a wet bar and overlooks the pool below.

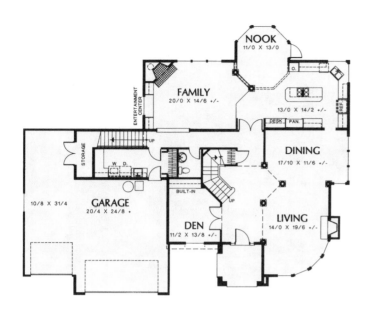

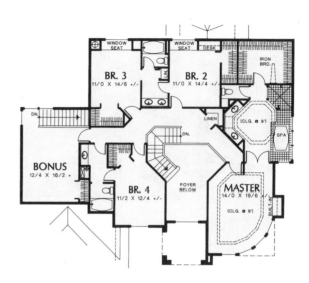

DESIGN HPT800066

First Floor: 1,912 square feet

Second Floor: 1,630 square feet

Total: 3,542 square feet

Bonus Space: 300 square feet

Width: 71'-0"

Depth: 58'-6"

This home's facade is all about strength—powerful columns support the entire home, as well as frame the grand entrance. A sunlit two-story foyer leads to all areas of this exceptional contemporary home. Enter the formal combined living and dining areas highlighted by glass walls and interior columns. The adjacent kitchen blends well with an octagonal nook and a family room with a corner fireplace. A den, a powder room and a utility room complete the first floor. Upstairs, the master suite features a curved-glass wall, a uniquely styled bath and a huge walk-in closet. Three additional bedrooms, two full baths and a bonus room complete the second floor.

Design HPT800067

First Floor: 2,870 square feet

Second Floor: 2,222 square feet

Total: 5,092 square feet

Width: 93'-4"
Depth: 82'-8"

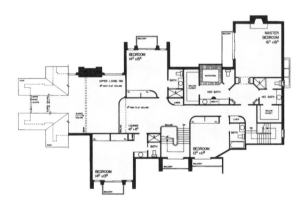

Semi-circular arches complement the strong linear rooflines and balconies of this exciting contemporary home. The first floor is filled with well-planned amenities for entertaining and relaxing. The foyer opens to a step-down living room with a dramatic sloped ceiling, a fireplace and four sliding glass doors that access the front courtyard and two terraces. A tavern with a built-in wine rack and an adjacent butler's pantry are ideal for entertaining. The family room features a fireplace, sliding glass doors and a handy snack bar. The kitchen allows for meal preparation, cooking and storage within a step of the central work island. Three second-floor bedrooms, each with a private bath and a balcony, are reached by either of two staircases. The master suite, with two baths and walk-in closets, a whirlpool tub and a fireplace, adds the finishing touch to this memorable home.

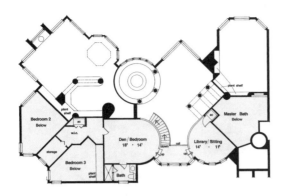

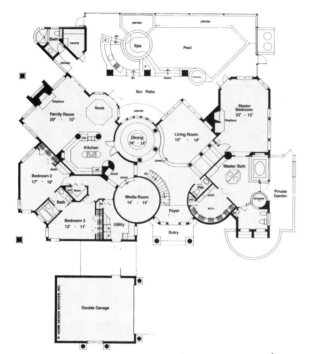

Design HPT800068

First Floor: 3,236 square feet
Second Floor: 494 square feet
Total: 3,730 square feet

Width: 80'-0"
Depth: 89'-10"

If you want to build a non-traditional home that is light years ahead of most other designs, yet addresses every need for your family, this showcase home is for you. From the moment you walk in, you are confronted with wonderful interior architecture that reflects modern, yet refined taste. The exterior says contemporary; the interior creates special excitement. Note the special rounded corners found throughout the home and the many amenities. The master suite is especially appealing with a fireplace and grand bath. Upstairs are a library/sitting room and a very private den or guest bedroom.

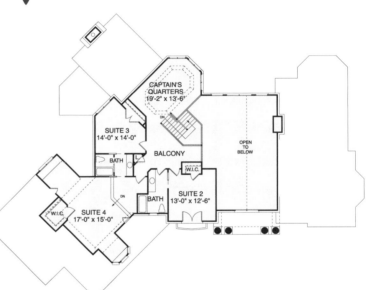

DESIGN HPT800069

First Floor: 2,943 square feet

Second Floor: 1,510 square feet

Total: 4,453 square feet

Width: 104'-2"
Depth: 78'-1"

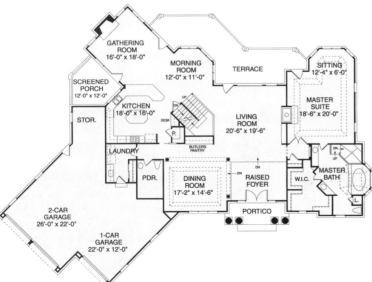

Interesting dormers and an amazing columned entry make this home quite unforgettable. The portico leads to the elegantly raised foyer and is framed by the columned dining room and spacious living room which leads to the rear terrace and offers a beautiful view of the backyard. The morning room is made up of a wall of windows, which flood the interior of the kitchen and gathering room with sunlight. The gathering room features a warming hearth for those few months out of the year where the only thing to do is curl up in front of the toasty fire. The kitchen offers a snack bar and plenty of counter space. The master suite offers a lavish sitting room and His and Hers walk-in closets. Two suites and a captain's quarters are located on the second level of this home for the ultimate in sleeping comfort.

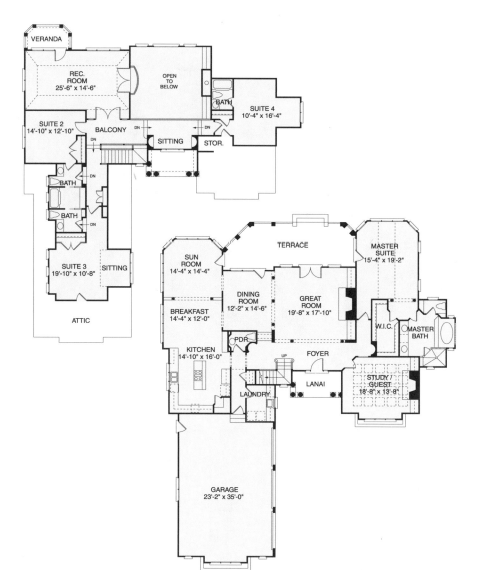

VERANDA

REC. ROOM
25'-6" x 14'-6"

OPEN TO BELOW

BATH

SUITE 4
10'-4" x 16'-4"

SUITE 2
14'-10" x 12'-10"

BALCONY

DN

DN

SITTING

DN

STOR.

BATH

DN

BATH

DN

SUITE 3
19'-10" x 10'-8"

SITTING

ATTIC

SUN ROOM
14'-4" x 14'-4"

TERRACE

MASTER SUITE
15'-4" x 19'-2"

DINING ROOM
12'-2" x 14'-6"

GREAT ROOM
19'-8" x 17'-10"

BREAKFAST
14'-4" x 12'-0"

W.I.C.

MASTER BATH

KITCHEN
14'-10" x 16'-0"

PDR.

UP

FOYER

LAUNDRY

LANAI

STUDY / GUEST
18'-8" x 13'-8"

GARAGE
23'-2" x 35'-0"

DESIGN HPT800070

First Floor: 2,577 square feet

Second Floor: 1,703 square feet

Total: 4,280 square feet

Width: 73'-2"
Depth: 86'-9"

Beautiful pedimented arches and various rooflines match the exquisite stucco exterior of this home. The two-story columns create a majestic aura which surrounds the home. The foyer extends to the great room which features arched entries and a relaxing fireplace. French doors lead guests and homeowners from the comforts of the great room to the excitement of the terrace. The dining room is well-situated from the U-shaped island kitchen. The ribbons of windows in the breakfast and sun rooms light the interior of the home dramatically. The master suite is complete with a fabulous walk-in closet and bath. A study/guest room is accented perfectly with a fireplace of its own. Three suites and a recreation room with a balcony comprise the second level.

ON THE WATERFRONT

Design HPT800071

First Floor: 3,555 square feet

Second Floor: 250 square feet

Total: 3,805 square feet

Bonus Space: 490 square feet

Width: 99'-8"

Depth: 78'-8"

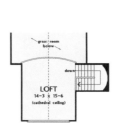

LOFT
14-3 x 15-6
(cathedral ceiling)

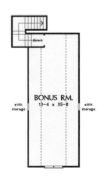

BONUS RM.
13-4 x 35-8

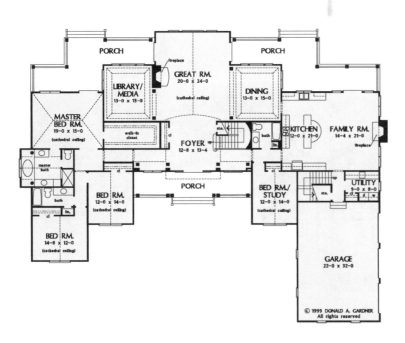

This extraordinary four-bedroom estate features gables with decorative wood brackets, arched windows and a stone-and-siding facade for undeniable Craftsman character. At the heart of the home, a magnificent cathedral ceiling adds space and stature to the impressive great room, which accesses both back porches. Sharing the great room's cathedral ceiling, a loft makes an excellent reading nook. Tray ceilings adorn the dining room and library/media room, while all four bedrooms enjoy cathedral ceilings. A sizable kitchen is open to a large gathering room for ultimate family togetherness. The master suite features back-porch access, a lavish private bath and an oversized walk-in closet. A spacious bonus room is located over the three-car garage for further expansion.

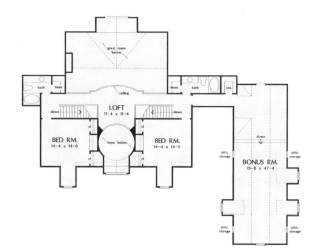

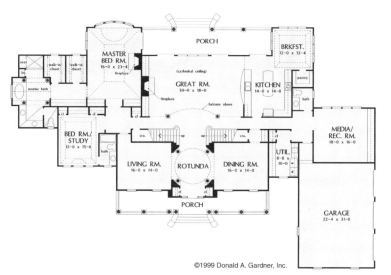

©1999 Donald A. Gardner, Inc.

Design HPT800072

First Floor: 3,732 square feet
Second Floor: 1,080 square feet
Total: 4,812 square feet

Bonus Space: 903 square feet
Width: 108'-4"
Depth: 73'-6"

A stunning combination of both country and traditional exterior elements creates a timeless facade for this exquisite estate home. A dramatic two-story rotunda makes a grand first impression, followed by equally impressive dual staircases and a large great room with cathedral ceiling and overlooking curved balcony and loft. The spacious kitchen easily serves the dining room, breakfast area, and great room. Note the walk-in pantry. The media/rec room features a wall of built-in cabinets to house television and stereo equipment. More oasis than bedroom, the master suite is amplified by a deep tray ceiling and enjoys a fireplace, built-in dressing cabinetry, His and Hers walk-in closets and a luxurious bath with every amenity. Two bedrooms, two baths and an oversized bonus room are on the second floor.

DESIGN HPT800073

Square Footage: 6,418

Finished Basement: 2,803 square feet
Width: 98'-0"
Depth: 94'-0"

This home is perfect for a hillside, lakeside or oceanside lot. It includes two very open levels with plenty of amenities to please the entire family. On the first floor is a huge, open kitchen with two islands. A spacious lodge room has sliding doors to the rear screened porch for the ultimate in vacationing, even at your own home. The dining hall is conveniently placed near the kitchen at the back of the home—where visions of the backyard entertain guests during the meal. The master bedroom is complete with French doors to the covered rear porch and a spacious walk-in closet. A wealth of recreation areas—from the driving range to the exercise room to the home theater—will provide enjoyment for the whole family.

Old World Splendor
Dignified, refined European estates

Design HPT800086, see page 117

DESIGN HPT800075

First Floor: 3,736 square feet
Second Floor: 2,264 square feet
Total: 6,000 square feet

Attic Storage: 644 square feet
Width: 133'-4"
Depth: 65'-5"

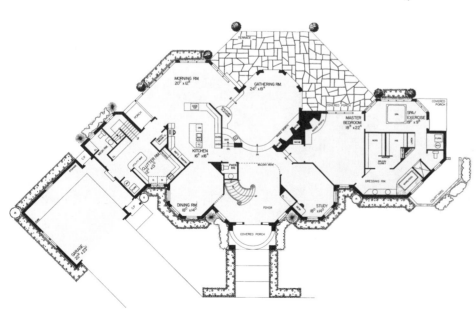

The distinctive covered entry to this stunning manor, flanked by twin turrets, leads to a gracious foyer with impressive fanlights. The plan opens from the foyer to a formal dining room, a study and a step-down gathering room. The spacious kitchen has numerous amenities, including an island work station and a built-in desk. The adjacent morning room and the gathering room, with a wet bar and a raised-hearth fireplace, are bathed in light and open to the terrace for outdoor entertaining. The luxurious and secluded master suite includes two walk-in closets, a dressing area and an exercise area with a spa. The second floor features four bedrooms and an oversized activities room with a fireplace and a balcony. Unfinished attic space can be completed to your specifications.

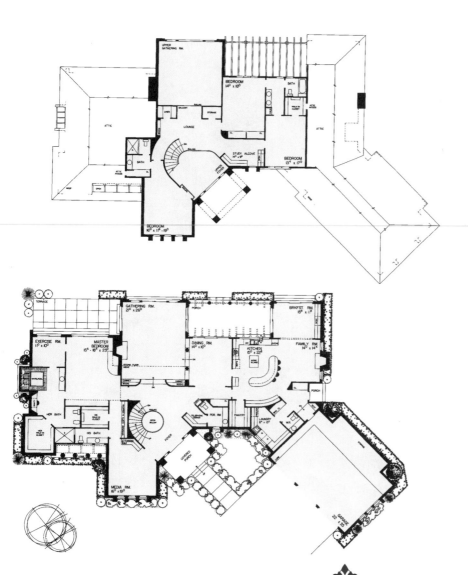

DESIGN HPT800076

First Floor: 4,222 square feet
Second Floor: 1,726 square feet
Total: 5,948 square feet

Width: 126'-5"
Depth: 78'-9"

This plan weds clean, contemporary design with a hint of French details to produce a spectacular home. The giant arched entry opens to a foyer with a magnificent curved stairway. Proceed further to the sunken gathering room with sliding glass doors and fireplace. A covered porch in the rear is accessed from the dining room and a huge living area that holds the kitchen (note the curved bar), family room with a fireplace, and breakfast room with a built-in desk. The master suite dominates one wing of the first floor and is highlighted by an exercise room, whirlpool, and His and Hers baths and closets. Adjacent is the media room with a wet bar and built-in bookcase. A relaxing lounge area on the second floor overlooks the gathering room and provides a central hall for three bedrooms and two full baths. Take note of the study alcove located nearby.

DESIGN HPT800077

First Floor: 4,786 square feet

Second Floor: 1,842 square feet

Total: 6,628 square feet

Width: 133'-8"
Depth: 87'-10"

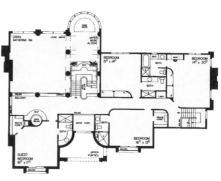

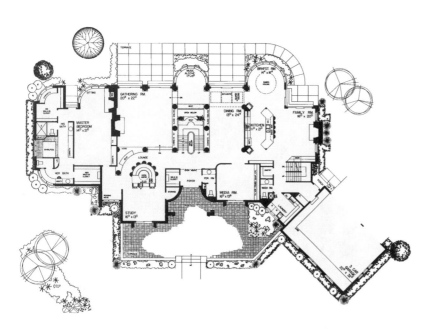

Graceful window arches soften the massive chimneys and hipped roof of this grand European manor that dazzles with French highlights. Inside, a two-story gathering room is just two steps down from the adjacent lounge with an impressive wet bar and a semi-circular music alcove. This area is reserved for elegant entertaining or decadent relaxation. The highly efficient galley-style kitchen overlooks the family-room fireplace and spectacular windowed breakfast room. The rear terrace is perfect for outdoor entertaining. The master suite is a private retreat with a fireplace and a wood box tucked into the corner of its sitting room. Separate His and Hers baths and dressing rooms guarantee plenty of space and privacy. A large, built-in whirlpool tub adds the final touch. A garage and utility room make the floor plan more efficient. Upstairs, a second-floor balcony overlooks the gathering room below.

First Floor: 3,722 square feet
Second Floor: 1,859 square feet
Total: 5,581 square feet

Width: 127'-10"
Depth: 83'-9"

BALCONY

BEDROOM 5
12-8 X 13-6
9 FT CEILING

BATH 4

BEDROOM 4
15-0 X 14-0
9 FT CEILING

GAME ROOM
19-0 X 26-4
9 FT CEILING

OPEN TO GREAT ROOM BELOW

ATTIC

ATTIC

BATH

BALCONY

BEDROOM 2
13-0 X 14-0
9 FT CEILING

OPEN TO ENTRY BELOW

BEDROOM 3
14-6 X 18-6
9 FT CEILING

BATH 3

SUN ROOM
15-0 X 14-0

PORCH

BRKFST AREA
13-6 X 13-6
9 FT CEILING

UTIL
7-8 X 10-4

ADDITIONAL GARAGE
35-0 X 40-0
10 FT CEILING

MASTER BEDROOM
19-0 X 17-8
11 FT CEILING

PORCH

LINEN

SIDE PORCH

SITTING
13-0 X 7-0
9 FT CEILING

DRESSING AREA
10-0 X 10-0
9 FT CEILING

GREAT ROOM
24-0 X 23-6
2 STORY CEILING

KITCHEN
19-0 X 21-6
9 FT CEILING

DOUBLE GARAGE
21-6 X 24-4
10 FT CEILING

HIS CLOSET

MASTER BATH
9 FT CEILING

HER CLOSET

PWD

PANTRY

STUDY
14-8 X 13-4
10 FT CEILING

ENTRY
2 STORY CEILING

DINING ROOM
13-6 X 18-4
10 FT CEILING

STORAGE
5-0 X 9-6

MECHANICAL

SINGLE GARAGE
11-0 X 24-0
9 FT CEILING

PORCH

A richly detailed entrance sets the elegant tone of this luxurious design. Rising gracefully from the two-story foyer, the staircase is a fine prelude to the great room beyond, where a fantastic span of windows on the back wall overlooks the rear grounds. The dining room is located off the entry and has a lovely coffered ceiling. The kitchen, breakfast room and sun room are conveniently grouped for casual entertaining. The elaborate master suite enjoys a coffered ceiling, private sitting room and spa-style bath. The second level consists of four bedrooms with private baths and a large game room featuring a rear stair.

DESIGN HPT800079

First Floor: 2,997 square feet

Second Floor: 983 square feet

Total: 3,980 square feet

Playroom: 208 square feet

Width: 89'-4"

Depth: 71'-0"

Corner quoins and arched windows make this a delicate but powerful home. The distinctive covered entry to this stunning manor leads to a gracious entry with impressive two-story semi-circular fanlights. The entry leads to a study, formal living and dining rooms and the master suite. Fireplaces can be enjoyed in both the family room and the living room. The numerous amenities in the kitchen include an island workstation and built-in pantry. The breakfast room features a cone ceiling. The luxurious master bath, secluded in its own wing, is complete with a covered patio. The master bedroom has a huge walk-in closet. Upstairs are three bedrooms, two baths and a future playroom area.

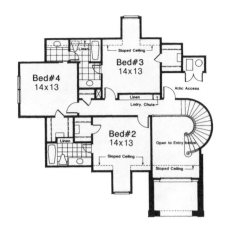

Bed#4
14x13

Bed#3
14x13

Linen

Sloped Ceiling

Attic Access

Linen

Lndry. Chute

Bed#2
14x13

Open to Entry Below

Linen

Sloped Ceiling

Sloped Ceiling

DESIGN HPT800083

First Floor: 2,728 square feet

Second Floor: 1,008 square feet

Total: 3,736 square feet

Width: 70'-0"
Depth: 56'-7"

Cast-stone arches, dentiled eaves and brick quoins harmonize on the facade of this traditional European design. A breathtaking, two-story entry reveals a curving stairway and balcony. The adjoining open spaces of the formal dining room and living room with a brick fireplace offer warm hospitality to guests. The family room provides another fireplace, a cathedral ceiling and access to the covered patio. To the front of the home, a study offers built-in bookshelves. The master suite features a pampering bath with dual vanities, a large tub and a private water closet. Three family bedrooms, each with a walk-in closet and access to a full bath, are located upstairs. A three-car garage is located at the rear of the home.

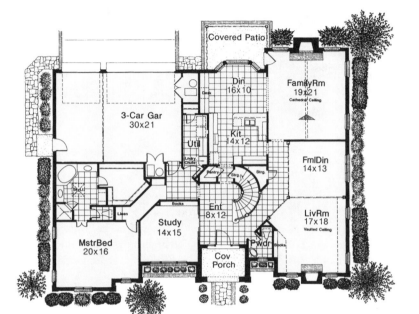

Covered Patio

3-Car Gar
30x21

Din
16x10

FamilyRm
19x21
Cathedral Ceiling

Kit
14x12

Util

Lndry
Chute

FmlDin
14x13

Pantry   Strg.   Strg.

Books

Ent
8x12

LivRm
17x18
Vaulted Ceiling

Linen

Study
14x15

Pwdr

Books

MstrBed
20x16

Cov
Porch

DESIGN HPT800082

First Floor: 2,814 square feet

Second Floor: 1,231 square feet

Total: 4,045 square feet

Width: 98'-0"
Depth: 45'-10"

Georgian design is the byword of estate living. It speaks of aristocracy and high society. And yet, it is never overstated or trite. This very formal Georgian was designed to be admired, but also to be lived in. It features handsome formal areas in a living room and formal dining room, but also an oversized family room with a focal fireplace. The master suite is on the first floor, as is popular with most homeowners today. Besides its wealth of amenities, it is located near a cozy study. Don't miss the private patio and sitting area in the master bedroom. Upstairs, there are four family bedrooms with great closet space. A three-car garage has space for a golf cart and a work bench.

SUITE 1
16'-0" x 15'-10"

W.I.C.

BATH

UP

BONUS
ROOM
19'-0" x 16'-0"

STOR.

BATH

W.I.C.

GALLERY

DN

DN

DN

BATH

W.I.C.

DN

UNFIN.
STOR.

SUITE 2
15'-3" x 15'-5"

OPEN
TO
BELOW

SUITE 3
15'-3" x 14'-5"

PLANTER

DECK

DEN
16'-2" x 19'-10"

SCREENED
PORCH

BREAKFAST
14'-6" x 14'-10"

GATHERING
ROOM
21'-3" x 20'-6"

MASTER
SUITE
22'-8" x 15'-0"

KITCHEN
18'-0" x 16'-0"

W.I.C.

PANT.

UP

BATH

LAUN.

DESK

UP

MASTER
BATH

PDR.

DINING
ROOM
15'-6" x 14'-2"

FOYER

STUDY/
GUEST
15'-3" x 14'-2"

LOGGIA

2-CAR
GARAGE
23'-6" x 22'-6"

1-CAR
GARAGE
19'-6" x 12'-6"

DESIGN HPT800080

First Floor: 3,487 square feet

Second Floor: 1,945 square feet

Total: 5,432 square feet

Bonus Space: 951 square feet
Width: 82'-4"
Depth: 105'-10"

This mystic European estate will enchant your lifestyle forever. Corner quoins, columns and a Palladian window over the balcony set this home apart from the rest. The loggia leads through the foyer—which is flanked by the dining room and study, both of which feature cozy fireplaces—to the gathering room where another fireplace can be found. The U-shaped kitchen is open to the den and breakfast room. The master suite has two walk-in closets and a master bath with dual vanities. Three suites—each with their own bath—a bonus room and storage space can be found on the second level.

DESIGN HPT800081

First Floor: 2,751 square feet
Second Floor: 1,185 square feet
Total: 3,936 square feet

Playroom: 289 square feet
Width: 79'-0"
Depth: 66'-4"

A grand brick facade, this home boasts muntin windows, multi-level rooflines, cut-brick jack arches and a beautifully arched entry. A cathedral-ceilinged living room, complete with fireplace, and a family dining room flank the twenty-foot high entry. Relax in the family room, mix a drink from the wet bar and look out through multiple windows to the covered veranda. A luxurious master suite includes a windowed sitting area looking over the rear view, private patio, full bath boasting a ten-foot ceiling and a spacious walk-in closet. On the second level, the three high-ceilinged bedrooms share two full baths and a study area with a built-in desk.

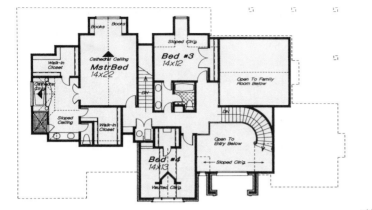

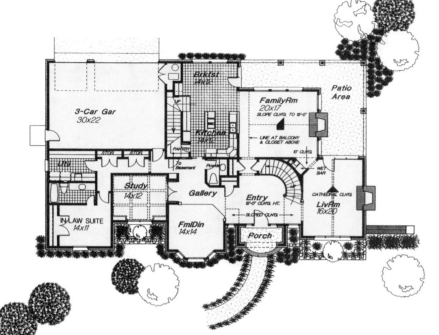

DESIGN HPT800084

First Floor: 2,506 square feet
Second Floor: 1,415 square feet
Total: 3,921 square feet

Width: 80'-5"
Depth: 50'-4"

Astately two-story home with a gracious, manor-like exterior features a large, arched entryway as its focal point. Excellent brick detailing and brick quoins help make this exterior one-of-a-kind. The large, two-story family area is adjacent to the living room with its cathedral ceiling and formal fireplace—a convenient arrangement for entertaining large groups, or just a cozy evening at home. A wrapping patio area allows for dining outdoors. The large kitchen is centrally located, with a second stairway leading to the second floor. The master suite features a volume ceiling and a sitting area overlooking the rear yard. The huge master bath includes two walk-in closets. The upper balcony overlooks the family area and the entryway.

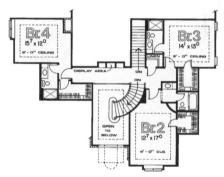

DESIGN HPT800085

First Floor: 2,839 square feet
Second Floor: 1,111 square feet
Total: 3,950 square feet

Width: 95'-9"
Depth: 70'-2"

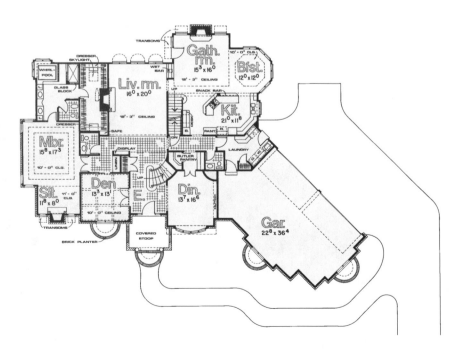

A two-story foyer introduces the formal living zones of this plan—a den with a ten-foot ceiling, a dining room with an adjoining butler's pantry, and a living room with a fireplace and a twelve-foot ceiling. For more casual living, the gathering room shares space with the octagonal breakfast area and the amenity-filled kitchen. Sleeping arrangements include a first-floor master suite, which offers a sitting area with a fireplace, a bath with a corner whirlpool tub and compartmented toilet, and an extensive closet. The second floor holds three bedrooms, each with a walk-in closet and private bath.

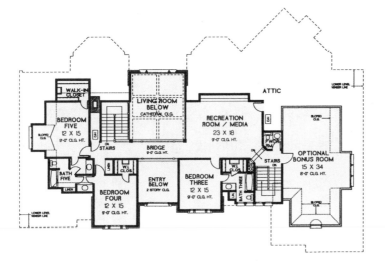

Design HPT800086

First Floor: 3,745 square feet
Second Floor: 1,643 square feet
Total: 5,388 square feet

Bonus Space: 510 square feet
Width: 100'-0"
Depth: 70'-1"

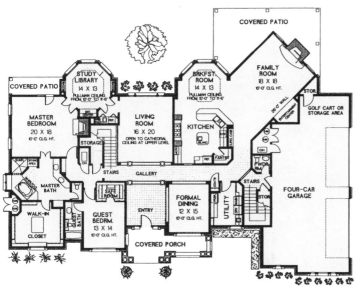

Steep rooflines and plenty of windows create a sophisticated aura around this home. Columns support the balconies above as well as the entry below. An angled family room featuring a fireplace is great for rest and relaxation. Snacks and sunlight are just around the corner with the nearby breakfast room and island kitchen. A ribbon of windows in the living room makes for an open feel. A bay-windowed study/library has two sets of French doors—one to the living room and one to the master suite. The master bedroom offers a bath with dual vanities and a spacious walk-in closet. Three family bedrooms are located on the upper level with a recreation/media room and an optional bonus room.

DESIGN HPT800087

First Floor: 3,300 square feet
Second Floor: 1,170 square feet
Total: 4,470 square feet

Width: 87'-0"
Depth: 82'-0"

The gracious exterior of this classic European-style home is accentuated by dual boxed windows, dramatically curved stairs and a glassed entry decorated with tall columns. A grand foyer showcases the dining room and great room, which offers a fireplace and French doors opening to a rear terrace. A gourmet kitchen adjoins the breakfast room, also open to the terrace; just beyond, a corner fireplace warms the hearth room. The luxurious master suite provides a spacious walk-in closet and an opulent bath. Upstairs, a balcony overlooks the foyer and gallery. Three secondary bedrooms provide walk-in closets; one offers a private bath.

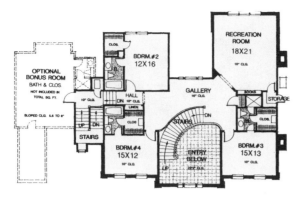

DESIGN HPT800088

First Floor: 3,599 square feet
Second Floor: 1,621 square feet
Total: 5,220 square feet

Bonus Space: 356 square feet
Width: 108'-10"
Depth: 53'-10"

A grand facade detailed with brick corner quoins, stucco flourishes, arched windows and an elegant entrance presents this home and preludes the amenities inside. A spacious foyer is accented by curving stairs and flanked by a formal living room and a formal dining room. For cozy times, a through-fireplace is located between a large family room and a quiet study. The master bedroom is designed to pamper, with two walk-in closets (one is absolutely huge), a two-sided fireplace sharing its heat with a bayed sitting area, and a lavish private bath filled with attractive amenities. Upstairs, three secondary bedrooms each have a private bath and walk-in closet. Also on this level is a spacious recreation room, perfect for a game room or children's playroom.

OLD WORLD SPLENDOR

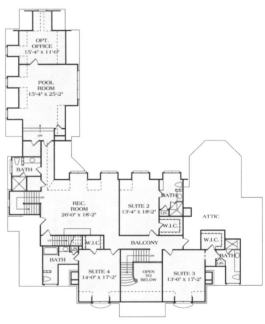

DESIGN HPT800089

First Floor: 3,420 square feet

Second Floor: 2,076 square feet

Total: 5,496 square feet

Bonus Space: 721 square feet

Width: 85'-6"

Depth: 102'-6"

Classic French elements along with style and balance give this home great curb appeal. The foyer leads to the gallery and on to the grand room, complete with its bank of windows, a fireplace and built-ins. Two more fireplaces can be found in the family room and the study, off the foyer. A secondary staircase leads from the kitchen/breakfast area to the recreational room on the second level. A pool room and office are tucked over the garage, and three bedroom suites and four full baths complete this floor. The master suite is located on the first level, allowing for privacy.

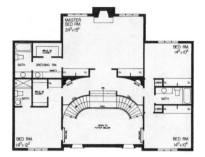

DESIGN HPT800090

First Floor: 2,345 square feet
Second Floor: 1,687 square feet
Total: 4,032 square feet

Width: 90'-4"
Depth: 44'-0"

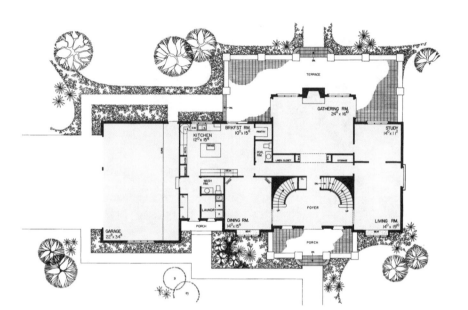

This best-selling French adaptation is highlighted by effective window treatments, delicate cornice detailing, appealing brick quoins and excellent proportions. The foyer is surrounded by dual staircases, which create an aura of royalty when one first enters the home. The gathering room features a grand fireplace and plenty of space to entertain guests. The living room and study are off to the right, each offering a ribbon of windows for superior natural lighting. The L-shaped kitchen extends to the breakfast room, where sliding doors access the backyard. Upstairs, a deluxe master bedroom suite is lavish in its efforts to pamper you. Three secondary bedrooms share this level; one includes its own bath and a walk-in closet; the other two bedrooms share a full bath.

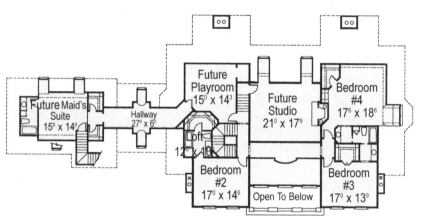

Future Maid's Suite
15⁰ x 14⁰

Hallway
27⁶ x 6⁰

Future Playroom
15⁰ x 14³

Future Studio
21⁰ x 17⁹

Bedroom #4
17⁶ x 18⁶

Loft
12⁰ x 10⁰

Bedroom #2
17⁰ x 14⁶

Open To Below

Bedroom #3
17⁰ x 13⁹

DESIGN HPT800091

First Floor: 3,703 square feet
Second Floor: 1,427 square feet
Total: 5,130 square feet

Bonus Space: 1,399 square feet
Width: 125'-2"
Depth: 58'-10"

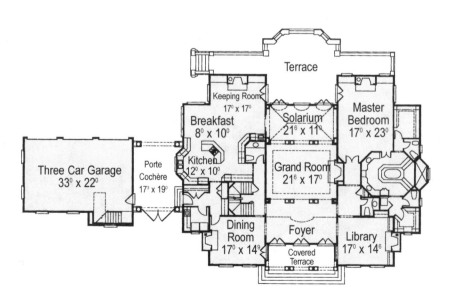

Three Car Garage
33⁰ x 22⁰

Porte Cochère
17³ x 19⁰

Terrace

Keeping Room
17⁰ x 17⁰

Breakfast
8⁰ x 10⁰

Kitchen
12⁰ x 10⁰

Solarium
21⁶ x 11⁰

Master Bedroom
17⁰ x 23⁰

Grand Room
21⁶ x 17⁰

Dining Room
17⁰ x 14⁹

Foyer

Library
17⁰ x 14⁶

Covered Terrace

This magnificent estate is detailed with exterior charm: a porte cochere connecting the detached garage to the house, a covered terrace and oval windows. The first floor consists of a lavish master suite, a cozy library with a fireplace, a grand room/solarium combination and an elegant formal dining room with another fireplace. Three bedrooms dominate the second floor—each features a walk-in closet. For the kids, there is a playroom and up another flight of stairs is a room for future expansion into a deluxe studio with a fireplace. Over the three-car garage, there is room for a future mother-in-law or maid's suite. This home is designed with a walkout basement foundation.

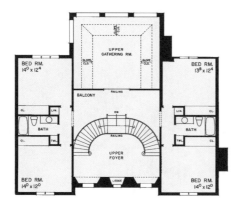

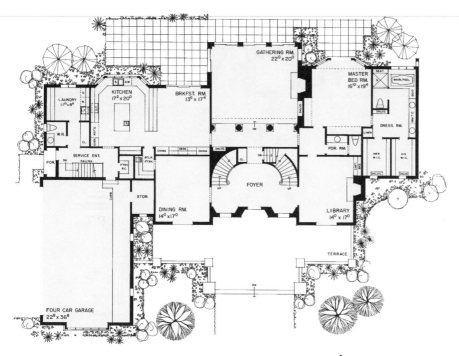

DESIGN HPT800092

First Floor: 3,350 square feet
Second Floor: 1,298 square feet
Total: 4,648 square feet

Width: 97'-0"
Depth: 74'-4"

Reminiscent of a Mediterranean villa, this grand manor is a show-stopper on the outside and a comfortable residence on the inside. An elegant receiving hall boasts a double staircase and is flanked by the formal dining room and the library. A huge gathering room at the back is graced by a fireplace and a wall of sliding glass doors to the rear terrace. The master bedroom resides on the first floor for privacy. With a lavish bath to pamper you and His and Hers walk-in closets, this suite will be a delight to retire to each evening. Upstairs are four additional bedrooms with ample storage space, a large balcony overlooking the gathering room and two full baths.

DESIGN HPT800093

First Floor: 2,887 square feet

Second Floor: 1,387 square feet

Total: 4,274 square feet

Bonus Space: 517 square feet

Width: 102'-2"

Depth: 73'-5"

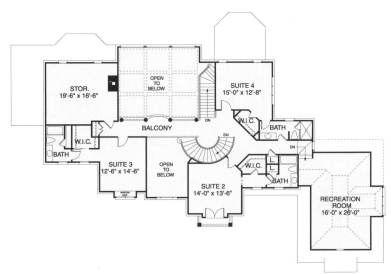

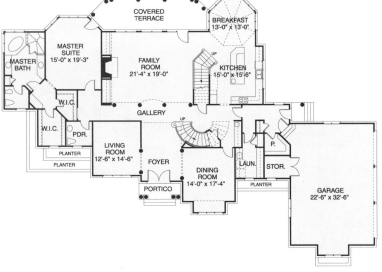

This European-style estate boasts impressive palatial luxury. The front portico leads inside to a spacious two-story foyer flanked on either side by formal living and dining rooms. A curved staircase cascading into the gallery hall spirals to the second floor. The two-story family room provides a formal fireplace. The master wing of the home features private access to the rear covered terrace, a lavish bath and two walk-in closets. The kitchen opens to a bayed breakfast room. Three additional family bedrooms are featured upstairs. The large recreation room is fun for the whole family.

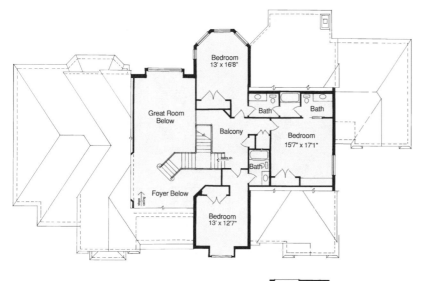

First Floor: 3,364 square feet
Second Floor: 1,198 square feet
Total: 4,562 square feet

Width: 98'-6"
Depth: 61'-5"

The richness of natural stone and brick sets the tone for the warmth and charm of this transitional home. The expansive entry is adorned with an angled stairway, a grand opening to the formal dining room and a view of the spectacular great room. A deluxe bath and a dressing area with a walk-in closet complement the master suite. The spacious island kitchen opens to the breakfast room and the cozy hearth room. Stairways in both the foyer and the kitchen provide convenient access to the second floor. A dramatic view greets you at the second-floor balcony. Two family bedrooms share a tandem bath that includes separate vanities, and a third bedroom holds a private bath.

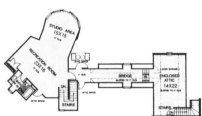

DESIGN HPT800096

First Floor: 5,152 square feet
Second Floor: 726 square feet
Total: 5,878 square feet

Width: 146'-7"
Depth: 106'-7"

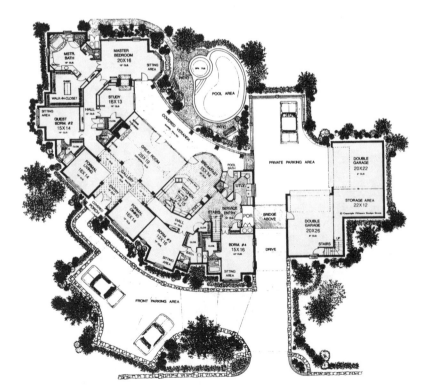

From the master bedroom suite to the detached four-car garage, this design will delight even the most discerning palates. While the formal living and dining rooms bid greeting as you enter, the impressive great room, with its cathedral ceiling, raised-hearth fireplace and veranda access will take your breath away. A gallery hall leads to the kitchen and the family sleeping wing on the right and to the study, guest suite and master suite on the left. The large island kitchen, with its sunny breakfast nook, will be a gourmet's delight. The master suite includes a bayed sitting area, a dual fireplace shared with the study, and a luxurious bath. Each additional bedroom features its own bath and sitting area. Upstairs is a massive recreation room with a sunlit studio area and a bridge leading to an attic over the garage.

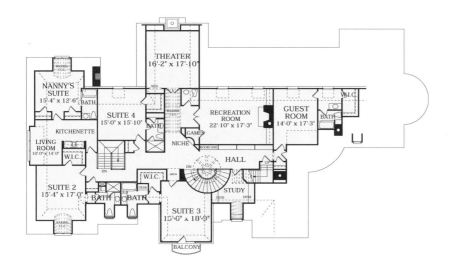

DESIGN HPT800095

First Floor: 4,565 square feet
Second Floor: 4,008 square feet
Total: 8,573 square feet

Width: 128'-4"
Depth: 71'-2"

Pinnacles and wide-open windows highlight the majesty of this European beauty. Stately French doors open from the portico to the foyer. The living room offers a chance to relax in front of the grand fireplace. Stone arches work well in the spacious kitchen and refined breakfast room. The kitchen is in direct connection with the family room, which also features a fireplace. The master suite privately accesses the rear covered lanai and includes other amenities such as separate baths, walk-in closets and a connected exercise area. The second floor could be an entirely separate living area with three suites, a nanny suite, theater, and recreation room.

DESIGN HPT800101

First Floor: 5,200 square feet

Second Floor: 4,177 square feet

Total: 9,377 square feet

Apartment: 792 square feet

Width: 155'-9"

Depth: 107'-11"

Gables, varied rooflines, interesting dormers, arched windows, a recessed entry—the detailing on this stone manor is exquisite! The foyer opens through arches to the formal dining room, an elegant stair hall and the grand room, with its fireplace, built-ins and French doors to the lanai. The informal zone includes a kitchen with an oversized work island and pantry, a breakfast nook and a family room with a fireplace and its own screened porch. An anteroom outside the master suite gives the homeowners added privacy and allows the option of a private entrance to the study. The master bath is loaded with extras, including a stairway to the upstairs exercise room. The second floor also offers a home theater and a home office, as well as four bedroom suites and a mother-in-law or maid's apartment.

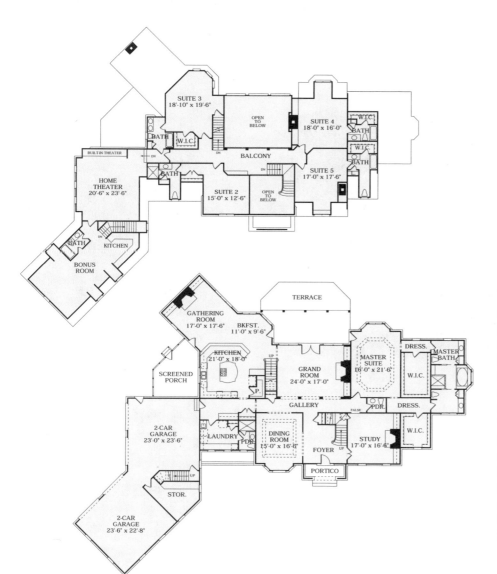

DESIGN HPT800097

First Floor: 3,767 square feet
Second Floor: 2,602 square feet
Total: 6,369 square feet

Bonus Space: 677 square feet
Width: 131'-0"
Depth: 99'-11"

Shake-covered dormers, segmented lintels and stone accents highlight this brick country home. Tall chimneys support three fireplaces—in the gathering room, the grand room and the study. Distinctive features include built-ins flanking the fireplaces, a large work island and walk-in pantry in the kitchen, and a laundry room with plenty of counter space for sorting and folding. The master suite offers private access to the terrace, two huge walk-in closets and His and Hers baths sharing only the tub and shower area. Three flights of stairs lead upstairs to four family bedroom suites with private baths, a home theater and bonus space over one of the two-car garages.

DESIGN HPT800099

First Floor: 3,560 square feet

Second Floor: 1,783 square feet

Total: 5,343 square feet

Bonus Space: 641 square feet

Width: 121'-2"

Depth: 104'-4"

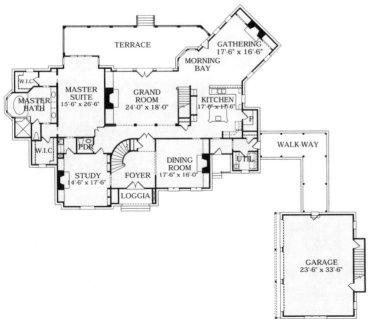

Multi-pane windows complement the porte cochere and dress up the natural stone facade of this French country estate. A two-story foyer leads to a central grand room with French doors to the terrace. A formal dining room to the front offers a fireplace. To the left, a cozy study with a second fireplace features built-in cabinetry and is close to a convenient powder room. The sleeping quarters offer luxurious amenities. The master bath includes a whirlpool tub in a bumped-out bay, twin lavatories and two walk-in closets. Upstairs, three suites, each with a walk-in closet and one with its own bath, share a balcony hall that leads to a home theater. A guest apartment over the garage will house visiting or live-in relatives, or may be used as a maid's quarters.

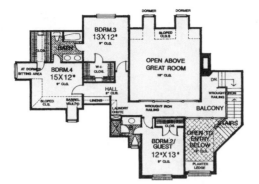

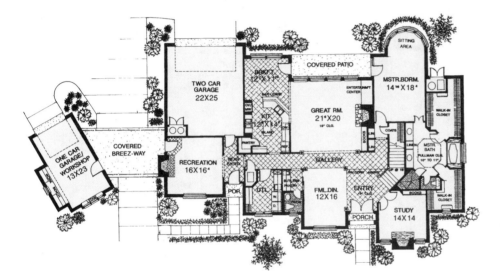

First Floor: 2,995 square feet
Second Floor: 1,102 square feet
Total: 4,097 square feet

Width: 120'-6"
Depth: 58'-8"

Stone pediments and a variety of window treatments ornament the facade of this grand European manor. Inside, to the right of the entry, the cozy study is accessed by double doors and includes a fireplace. The master suite, sharing the right wing of the home with the study, provides a private sitting area, a luxurious bath and two spacious walk-in closets. Central living spaces include the formal dining room, great room, breakfast nook and kitchen; a recreation room with a fireplace sits in the left wing. Upstairs, three additional bedrooms share a balcony that overlooks the great room.

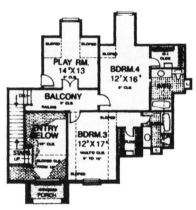

DESIGN HPT800098

First Floor: 2,994 square feet

Second Floor: 1,053 square feet

Total: 4,047 square feet

Width: 127'-10"
Depth: 61'-1"

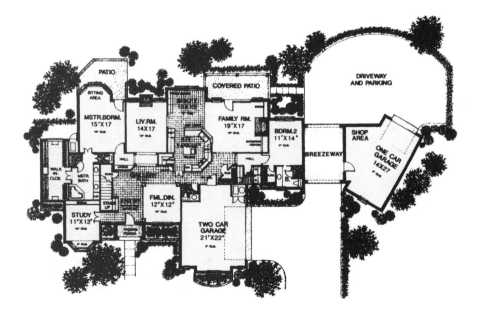

This European masterpiece is certainly refined and dignified in its own right. A grand entry signifies royalty and greatness. Inside, the foyer is flanked by a formal dining room and bayed study. The majestic living room has a grand fireplace and plenty of space for guests. The dining room offers a private exit to the rear covered patio. The master suite includes amenities such as a bayed sitting area, private access to a rear patio, a master bath with dual vanities and a spacious walk-in closet. The second level is comprised of a playroom and two family bedrooms, each with their own private bath.

Second floor plan labels:
- Sloping Ceiling
- Playrm. 13 x 19, Sloping Ceiling 6'-0" To 9'-0"
- Bath Three
- Bdrm. 3 12 X14, 9'-0" Clg. Ht.
- Closet
- Linen
- Bdrm. 4 12 x14, 9'-0" Clg. Ht.
- W.i. Clos.
- Attic Access
- Bath Four
- Study/Balcony 9'-0" Clg. Ht.
- W.i. Clos.
- Bath Two, Sloping Clg.
- Attic Access
- Dormer
- Bdrm. 2 14 X12, 9'-0" Clg. Ht.
- Entry Below 20' Clg. Ht.

DESIGN HPT800102

First Floor: 3,248 square feet
Second Floor: 1,426 square feet
Total: 4,674 square feet

Width: 99'-10"
Depth: 74'-10"

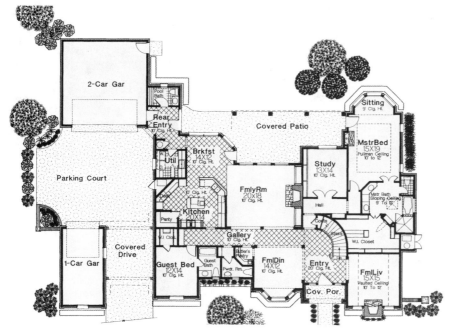

First floor plan labels:
- 2-Car Gar
- Pool Bath
- Rear Entry
- Covered Patio
- Sitting 9' Clg. Ht.
- MstrBed 15X19, Pullman Ceiling 10' to 12'
- Brkfst 14X12, 10' Clg. Ht.
- Util
- Study 13X14, 10' Clg. Ht.
- Parking Court
- FmlyRm 20X18, 10' Clg. Ht.
- Mstr Bath Sloping Ceiling 9' To 15'
- Kitchen 20X14
- Panty
- Hall
- Gallery 10' Clg. Ht.
- W.I. Closet
- Covered Drive
- Stairs
- Butler's Pantry
- FmlDin 14X12, 10' Clg. Ht.
- Entry 20' Clg. Ht.
- 1-Car Gar
- Guest Bed 12X14, 10' Clg. Ht.
- Guest Bath
- Pwdr. Rm.
- Cov. Por.
- FmlLiv 15X15, Vaulted Ceiling 10' To 12'

Multiple rooflines, a stone, brick and siding facade and an absolutely grand entrance combine to give this home the look of luxury. A striking family room showcases a beautiful fireplace framed with built-ins. The nearby breakfast room streams with light and accesses the rear patio. The kitchen features an island workstation, walk-in pantry and plenty of counter space. A guest suite is available on the first floor, perfect for when elderly members of the family visit. The first-floor master suite enjoys easy access to a large study, bayed sitting room and luxurious bath. Private baths are also included for each of the upstairs bedrooms.

DESIGN HPT800103

Square Footage: 4,270

Bonus Space: 774 square feet

Width: 112'-4"

Depth: 91'-3"

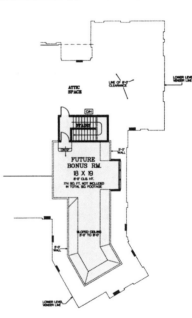

The subtle flaring of the eaves give this home a touch of warmth, while the pinnacles give this home strength. Grand windows shed light onto the one-story floor plan. French doors lead off the entry into the library/study. The living room features pullman ceilings and a grand fireplace. Another fireplace can be found in the family room, which showcases cathedral ceilings. The breakfast room is conveniently located near the kitchen as well as the rear covered patio. The master suite is loaded with many amenities, such as a His and Hers bath, walk-in closets, and a bayed sitting area. Three family bedrooms each come with separate baths and walk-in closets.

DESIGN HPT800104

First Floor: 4,958 square feet
Second Floor: 1,727 square feet
Total: 6,685 square feet

Width: 120'-9"
Depth: 114'-7"

Pinnacles on the rooftop are just the tip of the iceberg with this European beauty. A mixture of stone and brick complement this home's enchanted feel. French doors lead the homeowner or guest inside. A formal dining room and study/library flank the gallery. The formal living room features a fireplace and a great view of the covered rear patio into the backyard. The elegant kitchen offers an island and connection to the breakfast room. The relaxing family room also offers a fireplace. The guest bedroom is complete with a walk-in closet and sitting area. The master suite has a third fireplace as well as a private exercise room and grand master bath. Three family bedrooms and a recreation room with connection to a wood deck comprise the upper level of this home.

OLD WORLD SPLENDOR

DESIGN HPT800105

First Floor: 2,654 square feet

Second Floor: 1,013 square feet

Total: 3,667 square feet

Width: 75'-4"
Depth: 74'-2"

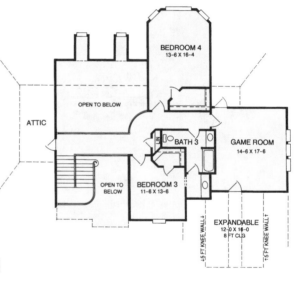

The flared eave, stone detail and shed dormer add class and sophistication to this home. The two-story living room creates an airy aura to the entire home. Two sets of French doors open to the rear covered porch. The same porch can be privately accessed from the spacious breakfast room and elegant master bedroom. A sitting room brightens the entire master bedroom. The kitchen has great service access to the breakfast, living, and dining rooms. A snack bar and island create an informal environment in the kitchen when appropriate. Two family bedrooms and a roomy game room are located on the second story. Please specify basement, crawlspace or slab foundation when ordering.

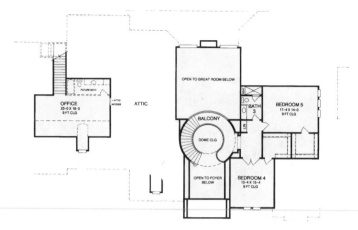

OFFICE
23-0 X 18-0
9 FT CLG

ATTIC

FUTURE BATH

ATTIC ACCESS

OPEN TO GREAT ROOM BELOW

BATH 3

BEDROOM 5
17-4 X 14-0
9 FT CLG

BALCONY
DOME CLG

OPEN TO FOYER BELOW

BEDROOM 4
13-4 X 15-4
9 FT CLG

DESIGN HPT800106

First Floor: 5,394 square feet
Second Floor: 1,305 square feet
Total: 6,699 square feet

Width: 124'-10"
Depth: 83'-2"

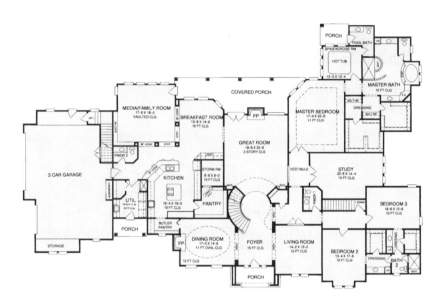

PORCH

POOL BATH

SPA/EXERCISE RM
HOT TUB
12-0 X 10-4

MASTER BATH
10 FT CLG

DRESSING

COVERED PORCH

MEDIA/FAMILY ROOM
17-6 X 18-0
VAULTED CLG

BREAKFAST ROOM
13-6 X 14-6
10 FT CLG

FP

MASTER BEDROOM
17-4 X 22-6
11 FT CLG

GREAT ROOM
19-6 X 22-6
2 STORY CLG

3 CAR GARAGE

PWDR 2

KITCHEN

STORM RM
8-6 X 8-0
10 FT CLG

VESTIBULE

STUDY
22-6 X 14-4
10 FT CLG

PWDR 1

BEDROOM 3
16-6 X 12-6
10 FT CLG

DOWN

UTIL
10-8 X 11-6
10 FT CLG

16-4 X 18-0
10 FT CLG

PANTRY

BUTLER PANTRY

PORCH

STORAGE

DINING ROOM
17-0 X 14-6
11 FT OVAL CLG
FP
10 FT CLG

FOYER
18 CLG

LIVING ROOM
14-2 X 15-2
10 FT CLG

BEDROOM 2
13-4 X 17-6
10 FT CLG

DRESSING

BATH 2
SEAT

PORCH

This European country favorite combines noble stonework and extraordinary siding detail. The expansive entry floods the foyer with natural light and heads under the balcony of the staircase into the open great room. A cozy breakfast room is just off the great room and is connected to the island kitchen, which features a butler's pantry that can be used to easily serve the formal dining room. A fireplace in the dining room will warm dinner guests. The master bedroom offers many amenities such as a spa and exercise room, dual walk-in closets and dressing rooms complete with built-ins, a whirlpool tub and access to a private porch. Two family bedrooms also have their own dressing rooms.

OLD WORLD SPLENDOR

COPYRIGHT LARRY E. BELK

Design HPT800107

First Floor: 3,033 square feet

Second Floor: 1,545 square feet

Total: 4,578 square feet

Width: 91'-6"
Depth: 63'-8"

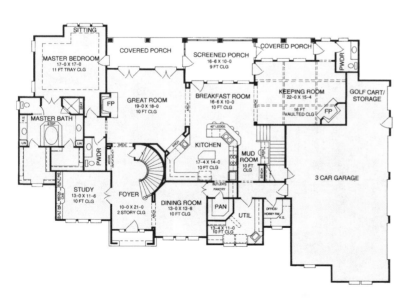

The details that make this Romanesque home amazing are the eyebrow dormers, arched trusses and pinnacle rooftop. The grand windows in the front flood the study and dining room with sunlight. Inside, through the foyer is the great room, featuring a fireplace and two sets of French doors exiting to the rear covered porch. The same porch can be easily accessed from the master bedroom. Within the master bedroom are two large walk-in closets open to the master bath, where two vanities and a whirlpool tub make living relaxing. The open kitchen is brightly lit from the breakfast room which is located just off the screened porch. Two family bedrooms and a game room are located on the second floor. Please specify basement, crawlspace or slab foundation when ordering.

DESIGN HPT800108

First Floor: 3,030 square feet
Second Floor: 848 square feet
Total: 3,878 square feet

Width: 88'-0"
Depth: 72'-1"

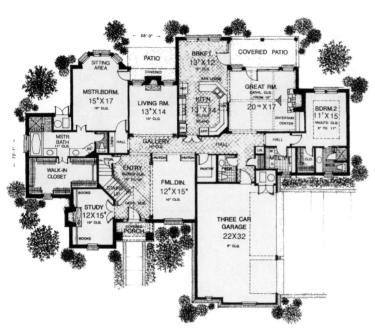

This dazzling and majestic European design features a stucco and stone facade, French shutters and castle-like rooflines. The entry is flanked by a study with a fireplace and a formal dining room. The formal living room with a fireplace is just across the gallery. The master wing is brightened by a bayed sitting area and features a private bath that extends impressive closet space. The island kitchen overlooks the breakfast and great rooms. A guest suite is located on the first floor for privacy, while two additional family bedrooms reside upstairs, along with a future playroom.

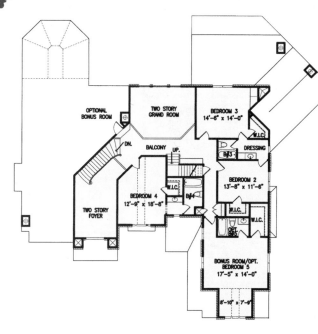

DESIGN HPT800109

First Floor: 3,121 square feet

Second Floor: 1,278 square feet

Total: 4,399 square feet

Bonus Room: 351 square feet

Width: 86'-7"

Depth: 81'-4"

This classic facade showcases a fabulous stone and brick combination. Windows abound on this home to make the exterior as lovely as the well-lit interior. The foyer leads through double doors into a lush library complete with a relaxing fireplace. The formal dining room is situated left of the kitchen with a butler's pantry located just around the corner. The kitchen is entirely open with plenty of counter space and two islands. The breakfast nook helps light up the family room and kitchen with the view of the covered rear porch and deck. The family room includes a fireplace, which creates a relaxing environment for quality family time. The lavish master suite is complete with dual vanities, walk-in closets and a comfortable sitting area. Four family bedrooms are located on the second floor.

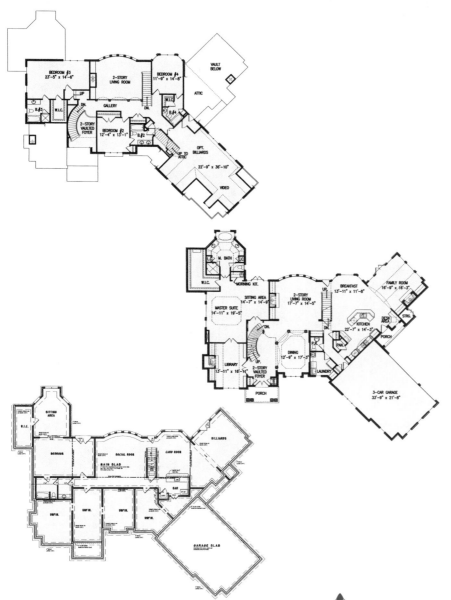

First Floor: 3,056 square feet
Second Floor: 1,307 square feet
Total: 4,363 square feet

Bonus Space: 692 square feet
Width: 94'-4"
Depth: 79'-2"

Arched windows lend this home a soft, but entirely noble, exterior. The stone and brick combination creates an aura of royalty. Through the decorative porch is the two-story vaulted foyer, separated from the formal dining area by arched columns. The two-story living room features a fireplace and wall of refined windows. The breakfast room is open to the kitchen, which features a snack bar and an island counter. The family room is angled to the right with a fireplace and French doors opening to the backyard. The master suite offers many lush amenities ranging from a sitting area to a morning kitchen. Three family bedrooms and a billiard room are found on the second floor.

OLD WORLD SPLENDOR

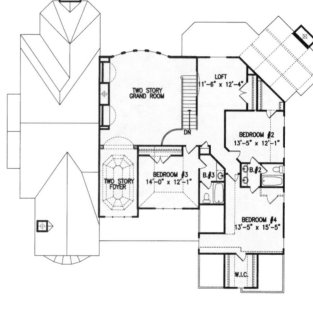

DESIGN HPT800110

First Floor: 2,729 square feet
Second Floor: 1,157 square feet
Total: 3,886 square feet

Width: 73'-11"
Depth: 70'-11"

Steep rooflines and grand windows lend this home its powerful exterior. Pedimented arches add sophistication and class. French doors lead to the foyer and into the grand room, which features a great view of the backyard as well as a warming fireplace. The master suite also features a fireplace in the sitting area. The master bath is arranged well with His and Hers walk-in closets included. The family room has yet another fireplace and is angled towards the breakfast nook and spacious kitchen. The formal dining area, defined by columns, is ideal for entertaining. Three family bedrooms are located on the second floor along with a loft.

Floor Plan Labels (Second Floor)

- TWO STORY COVERED VARANDA
- TWO STORY LIVING ROOM
- BEDROOM 2 17'-11" x 14'-0"
- BATH
- W.I.C.
- RETREAT 16'-5" x 12'-3"
- BALCONY
- W.I.C.
- BATH
- W.I.C.
- TWO STORY FOYER
- BEDROOM 3 15'-9" x 15'-5"
- BATH
- BEDROOM 4 12'-1" x 17'-3"
- BATH
- W.I.C.
- W.I.C.
- BATH
- BEDROOM 5 16'-11" x 14'-8"
- BATH

Floor Plan Labels (First Floor)

- MASTER BEDROOM 19'-9" x 21'-9" TRAY
- VAULTED KEEPING ROOM 18'-3" x 23'-9"
- TWO STORY COVERED VARANDA 24'-10" x 12'-6"
- DECK / PATIO
- M.BATH TRAY
- TWO STORY LIVING ROOM 15'-8" x 15'-5"
- KITCHEN
- P.R.
- PANTRY
- BREAKFAST 13'-11" x 11'-10"
- COVERED BREEZEWAY
- W.I.C.
- 16'-2" x 18'-2"
- FOURTH CAR GARAGE 16'-5" x 25'-4"
- GALLERY
- UP
- LAUNDRY
- DN
- VAULTED LIBRARY 14'-6" x 21'-5"
- TWO STORY FOYER
- DINING 15'-5" x 16'-7"
- PORCH
- THREE CAR GARAGE 23'-4" x 35'-1"

DESIGN HPT800111

First Floor: 3,559 square feet
Second Floor: 1,888 square feet
Total: 5,447 square feet

Retreat: 320 square feet
Width: 106'-6"
Depth: 89'-5"

This design is quite the view with all the wonderful windows and defined rooflines. Natural light flows through this home, making a very formal but comfortable environment. The two-story foyer leads into the two-story living room and provides a view of the covered porch. Three fireplaces can be found throughout this home—one in the keeping room, one in the living room and one in the library. The master bedroom is complete with dual vanities, roomy walk-in closets, and private access to the two-story covered porch. Three family bedrooms reside on the second floor. A retreat is also located on the second floor with private French-door access from below.

OLD WORLD SPLENDOR

DESIGN HPT800112

First Floor: 3,538 square feet

Second Floor: 1,540 square feet

Total: 5,078 square feet

Bonus Space: 524 square feet

Width: 96'-2"

Depth: 96'-8"

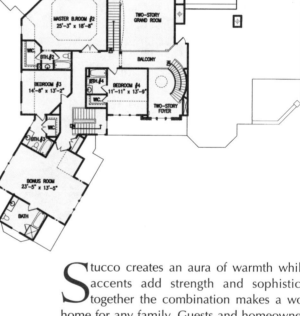

Stucco creates an aura of warmth while stone accents add strength and sophistication—together the combination makes a wonderful home for any family. Guests and homeowners enter through French doors to the two-story foyer, then onto the rest of this magnificent home. Columns frame the formal dining room—sure to please all who enter. Natural light shines through the two-story grand room, which also features a fireplace for warmth all year round. The angled family room also features a fireplace and is located conveniently off the kitchen and bayed breakfast nook. The master suite accesses a private rear porch, and showcases a retreat and spacious walk-in closet. Another master bedroom is located on the second floor, as well as two family bedrooms and a bonus room.

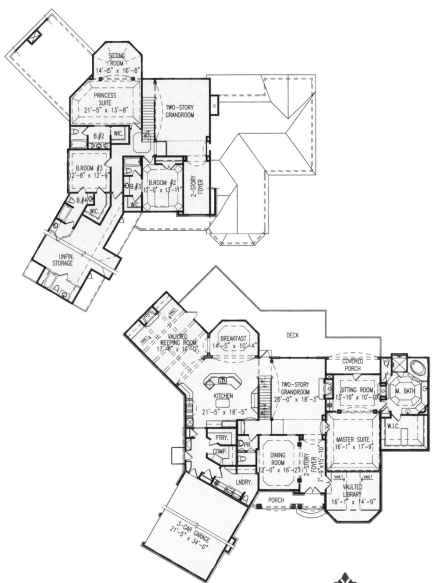

DESIGN HPT800113

First Floor: 3,348 square feet

Second Floor: 1,154 square feet

Total: 4,502 square feet

Storage Area: 723 square feet

Width: 91'-3"

Depth: 94'-6"

Multiple rooflines and window designs draw attention to this majestic home. This versatile design will fit in—while standing out—in any neighborhood. The grand entry features a two-story foyer and immediately takes the guest to the formal dining room, which is elegantly highlighted with a columned entry. The grand room features a fireplace and an expansive view of the backyard. The vaulted keeping room showcases another fireplace, which is placed at an angle so it can warm the breakfast nook and be viewed from the kitchen. The master suite privately accesses the rear covered porch and relishes in the comfort of a sitting room. Two family bedrooms and a princess suite are located on the second floor.

DESIGN HPT800114

First Floor: 2,340 square feet

Second Floor: 1,806 square feet

Total: 4,146 square feet

Basement: 1,608 square feet

Width: 117'-6"

Depth: 74'-5"

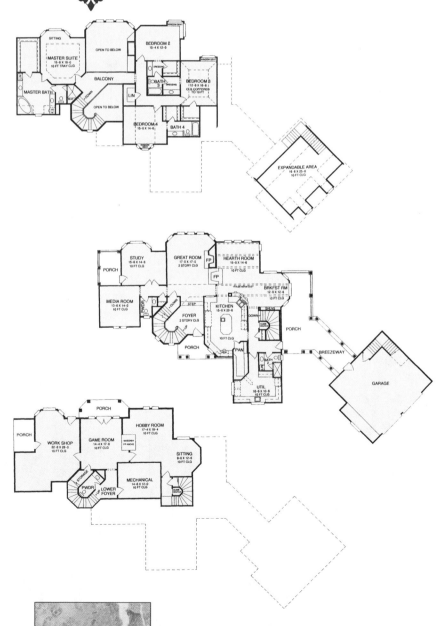

Full of amenities, this country estate includes a media room and a study. The two-story great room is perfect for formal entertaining. Family and friends will enjoy gathering in the large kitchen, the hearth room and the breakfast room. The luxurious master suite is located upstairs. Bedrooms 2 and 3 share a bath that includes dressing areas for both bedrooms. Bedroom 4 features a private bath. The detached garage is equipped with stairs to the expandable area above. The home features a rear stair complete with a dumbwaiter, which goes down to a walkout basement, where you'll find an enormous workshop, a game room and a hobby room. Please specify basement or slab foundation when ordering.

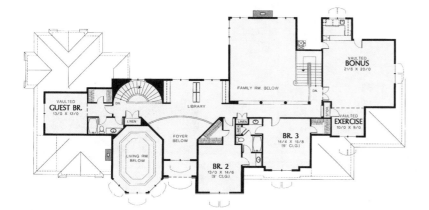

DESIGN HPT800115

First Floor: 3,833 square feet

Second Floor: 2,133 square feet

Total: 5,966 square feet

Bonus Space: 436 square feet

Width: 125'-6"

Depth: 80'-8"

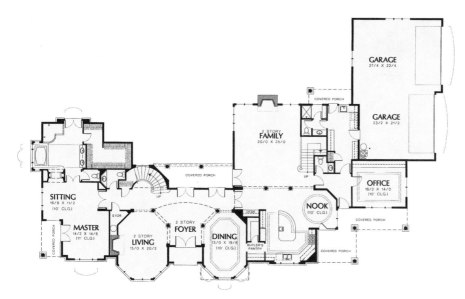

Stucco and stone details and multiple gables give this home a distinctive exterior. The striking glass-walled turret houses an elegant, octagonal two-story living room with a fireplace. The dining room, across the foyer, leads to the gourmet kitchen through a butler's pantry. The kitchen opens to the large family room and a breakfast nook with access to a covered porch. The master suite takes up the left wing of the house with its bumped-out garden tub, room-sized walk-in closet and private covered porch. Two staircases—a beautifully curved one in the foyer and one in the family room—lead upstairs, where three bedrooms share two baths along with an exercise room and a large bonus room over the garage.

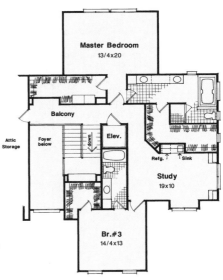

DESIGN HPT800116

First Floor: 2,192 square feet

Second Floor: 1,417 square feet

Total: 3,609 square feet

Width: 62'-0"

Depth: 64'-0"

A variety of textures, arches and angles adds interest to this impressive elevation. Inside, columns define the living areas, separating the living room from the foyer and the dining room, and marking the entrance to the breakfast area. The family room is a delight, with a wall of windows and a cheery fireplace. The family cook will enjoy the efficient island kitchen, with views of the back porch, a convenient butler's pantry and a spacious laundry room nearby. The deluxe master suite offers two immense walk-in closets and a bath that is sure to please.

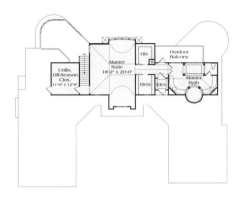

DESIGN HPT800117

First Floor: 2,971 square feet

Second Floor: 2,199 square feet

Third Floor: 1,040 square feet

Total: 6,210 square feet

Finished Basement: 1,707 square feet

Width: 84'-4"

Depth: 64'-11"

Symmetry and stucco present true elegance on the facade of this five-bedroom home and the elegance continues inside over four separate levels. Note the formal and informal gathering areas on the main level: the music room, the lake living room, the formal dining room and the uniquely shaped breakfast room. The second level contains three large bedroom suites—one with its own bath—a spacious girl's room for play time and an entrance room to the third-floor master suite. Lavish is the only way to describe this suite. Complete with His and Hers walk-in closets, a private balcony, an off-season closet and a sumptuous bath, this suite is designed to pamper the homeowner. In the basement is yet more room for casual get-togethers. Note the large sitting room as well as the hobby/crafts room. And tying it all together, an elevator offers stops at each floor.

DESIGN HPT800118

First Floor: 2,720 square feet
Second Floor: 1,412 square feet
Total: 4,132 square feet

Width: 73'-0"
Depth: 63'-0"

Corner quoins, arched windows and a hipped roofline decorate the facade of this European estate. A vaulted library/parlor sits to the left of the entry, while the formal dining room awaits to the right. Vaulted ceilings also enhance the family room, master bath, master-suite sitting area, and an upstairs loft area, while a two-story ceiling highlights the grand room. A bay window brightens the breakfast nook, which opens to a small side porch. Luxury abounds in the master suite with two walk-in closets, linen storage, and a bath with a raised tub, separate shower and plant shelves. Upstairs, find three bedrooms—one with a bay window and all with walk-in closets—and two full baths.

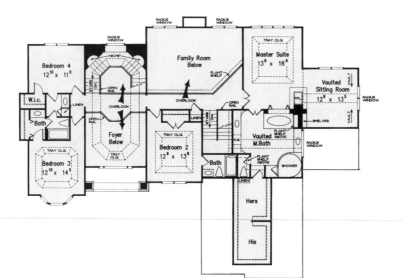

DESIGN HPT800119

First Floor: 2,190 square feet
Second Floor: 1,865 square feet
Total: 4,055 square feet

Width: 79'-0"
Depth: 60'-4"

This European-style home offers an array of stunning windows that serve both aesthetic and practical purposes. The accentuated foyer lends this home an overall elegant feel. Inside, the foyer leads to the grand staircase and balcony overlook above. A food-prep island defines the space between the breakfast area and the kitchen. The kitchen also contains dual ovens, extra counter space and a sizable pantry. The rambling master suite is located on the second floor—the official sleeping quarters—and features a sitting room, fireplace, full bath and two walk-in closets. Three family bedrooms complete the sleeping quarters. Please specify basement or slab foundation when ordering.

DESIGN HPT800120

First Floor: 2,420 square feet
Second Floor: 1,146 square feet
Total: 3,566 square feet

Width: 77'-8"
Depth: 50'-8"

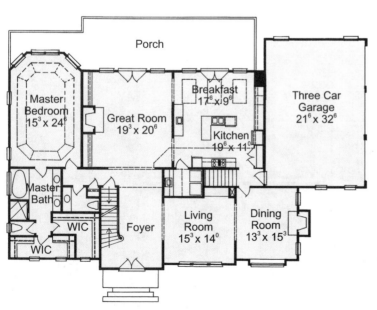

Multi-pane glass windows, double French doors and ornamental stucco detailing are complementary elements on the facade of this home. An impressive two-story foyer opens to the formal living and dining rooms. Natural light is available through the attractive windows in each room. The kitchen features a pass-through to the two-story great room and an adjoining skylit breakfast room. The first-floor master suite offers an elegant tray ceiling, a bath with twin vanities, a separate shower and tub, and two spacious walk-in closets. Upstairs, Bedroom 2 has its own bath and can be used as a guest suite. Two other bedrooms share a large bath that includes twin vanities. This home is designed with a walkout basement foundation.

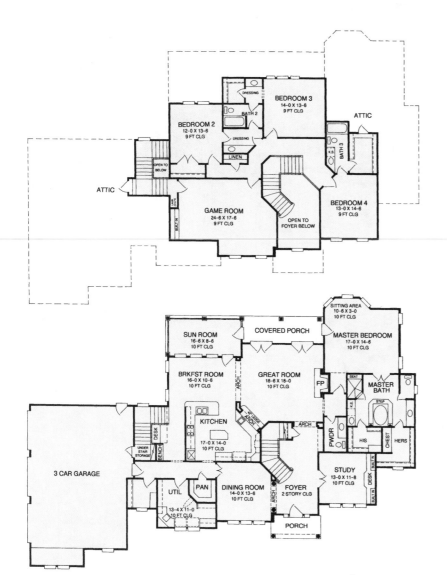

DESIGN HPT800121

First Floor: 2,608 square feet
Second Floor: 1,432 square feet
Total: 4,040 square feet

Width: 89'-10"
Depth: 63'-8"

A distinctively French flair is the hallmark of this European design. Inside, the two-story foyer provides views to the huge great room beyond. A well-placed study off the foyer provides space for a home office. The kitchen, breakfast room and sun room are adjacent to lend a spacious feel. The great room is visible from this area through decorative arches. The master suite includes a roomy sitting area and a lovely bath with a centerpiece whirlpool tub flanked by half-columns. Upstairs, Bedrooms 2 and 3 share a bath that includes separate dressing areas. Please specify crawlspace or slab foundation when ordering.

DESIGN HPT800122

First Floor: 3,721 square feet

Second Floor: 1,781 square feet

Total: 5,502 square feet

Width: 91'-6"

Depth: 82'-4"

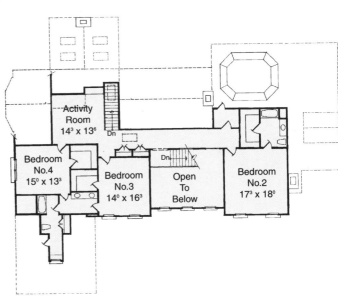

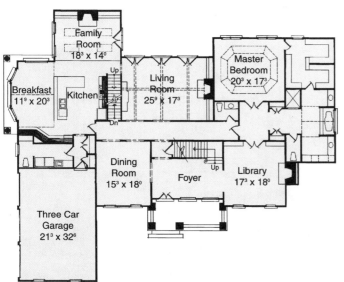

Rich in English flavor, this stucco beauty is bursting with expanses of glass and ornate details. The two-story foyer is flanked by a superb dining room and an elegant library. Beyond, the formal living room offers access to the patio and connects to the casual family room (note the skylights and fireplace here), breakfast room and kitchen. The master suite provides a splendid retreat with a tray ceiling, vaulted bath and patio access. Upstairs, three more bedrooms and an activity room share a back staircase to the kitchen and family room. Bedroom 2 has a private bath. This home is designed with a walkout basement foundation.

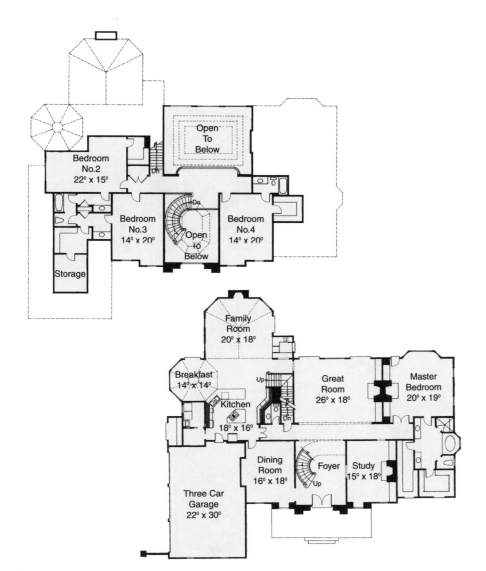

DESIGN HPT800123

First Floor: 3,568 square feet
Second Floor: 1,667 square feet
Total: 5,235 square feet

Width: 86'-8"
Depth: 79'-0"

The ornamental stucco detailing on this home creates an Old World Mediterranean charm and complements its strength and prominence. The two-story foyer with a sweeping curved stair opens to the large formal dining room and study. The master suite, offering convenient access to the study, is complete with a fireplace, His and Hers walk-in closets and a bath with twin vanities and a separate shower and tub. The two-story great room overlooks the rear patio. A large kitchen with an island workstation opens to an octagonal-shaped breakfast room and the family room. A staircase located off the family room provides additional access to the three second-floor bedrooms that each offer walk-in closets and plenty of storage. This home is designed with a walkout basement foundation.

DESIGN HPT800124

First Floor: 2,553 square feet
Second Floor: 1,370 square feet
Total: 3,923 square feet

Bonus Space: 280 square feet
Width: 74'-0"
Depth: 99'-4"

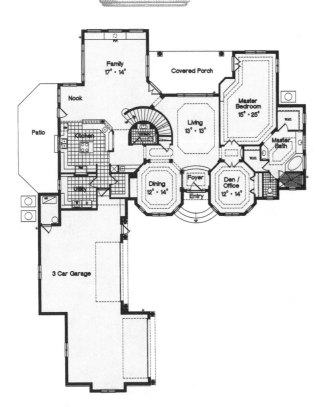

The excitement of this plan begins with its European-style elevation. The raised foyer welcomes guests into formal living and dining rooms, both with creative ceiling treatments. A home office is conveniently positioned near the master suite. The master bedroom features a tray ceiling and a sitting area. The master bath has His and Hers vanities and walk-in closets. The family room combines with a nook and island kitchen for casual living space. Note the hall to the three-car garage; it also leads to a huge laundry and a walk-in closet. Second-floor space includes two generous bedrooms with a shared bath, an activity room, a home theater and unfinished space that may become an additional bedroom.

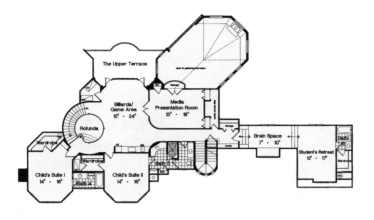

The Upper Terrace

Billiards/
Game Area
15' · 24'

Media
Presentation Room
13' · 18'

Rotunda

Wardrobe

Wardrobe

Brain Space
7' · 10'

Student's Retreat
12' · 17'

Bath 5

Bath 4

Child's Suite I
14' · 16'

Child's Suite II
14' · 16'

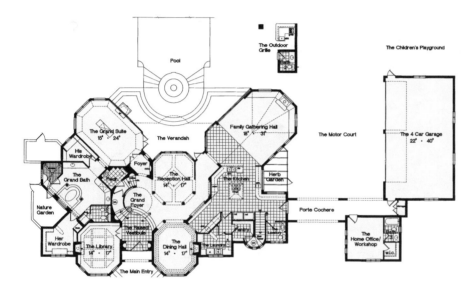

Pool

The Outdoor Grille

Bath

The Children's Playground

The Grand Suite
15' · 24'

Family Gathering Hall
18' · 31'

The Verandah

The Motor Court

The 4 Car Garage
22' · 40'

His Wardrobe

Foyer

The Grand Bath

The Reception Hall
14' · 17'

The Kitchen

Herb Garden

The Grand Foyer

Nature Garden

Porte Cochere

Her Wardrobe

The Raised Vestibule

The Library
14' · 17'

The Dining Hall
14' · 17'

Pantry

The Laundry

The Home Office/
Workshop

Bath

w.i.c.

The Main Entry

DESIGN HPT800125

First Floor: 3,874 square feet
Second Floor: 2,588 square feet
Total: 6,462 square feet

Home Office/Retreat: 1,117 square feet
Width: 137'-8"
Depth: 91'-7"

Everything you remember about French Chateau architecture is part of this magnificent estate home. From the opulent towers to the porte cochere—this is palatial living! An oversized front entry beckons your attention to the wonderful amenities inside: a raised, marble vestibule with a circular stair; a formal library and dining hall with views to the veranda and pool beyond; and a family gathering hall, open to the kitchen and connected to the outdoor grill. The master suite is embellished with a nature garden, His and Hers wardrobes, a fireplace and an elegant bath. Each of the family bedrooms features a private bath—one suite is reached via a bridge over the porte cochere. Other unique details include a wet bar in the game area, a sunset balcony, and a dual-use butler's pantry with a motorized screen to hide the bar pass-through to the reception hall and herb garden.

DESIGN HPT800126

First Floor: 4,508 square feet

Second Floor: 3,322 square feet

Total: 7,830 square feet

Width: 83'-0"
Depth: 77'-0"

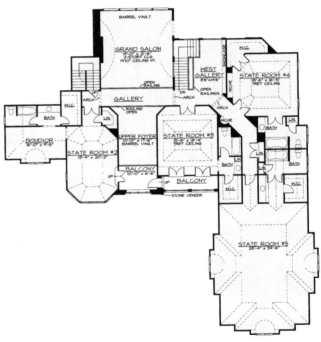

A stone-and-siding exterior, spires and interesting window details add to the elegance of this four-bedroom mansion. A keeping room with a pass-through to the kitchen and a fireplace with a built-in wood box, and a formal dining room with a fireplace on the first floor allow plenty of social possibilities. Separate guest quarters with a full bath, a lounge area and an upstairs studio, which is connected to the main house by a gallery, further enhance this home's livability. Four bedrooms with two full baths are found on the second floor, including the master suite with a fireplace.

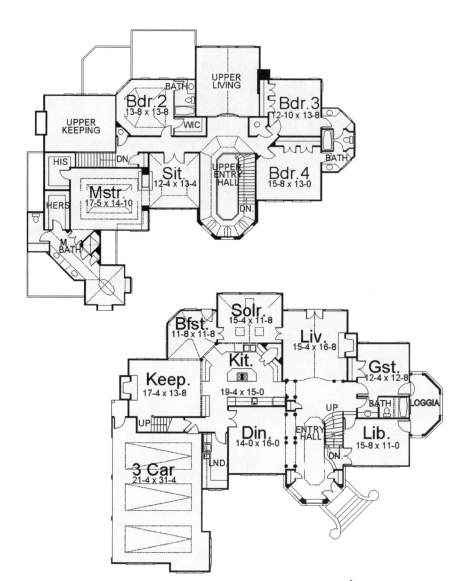

Design HPT800I27

First Floor: 2,559 square feet
Second Floor: 2,140 square feet
Total: 4,699 square feet

Width: 80'-0"
Depth: 67'-0"

Accommodate your life's diverse pattern of formal occasions and casual times with this spacious home. The exterior of this estate presents a palatial bearing, while the interior is both comfortable and elegant. Formal areas are graced with amenities to make entertaining easy. Casual areas are kept intimate, but no less large. The solarium serves both with skylights and terrace access. Guests will appreciate a private guest room and a bath with loggia access on the first floor. Family bedrooms and the master suite are upstairs. Note the gracious ceiling treatment in the master bedroom, its sitting room and Bedroom 2.

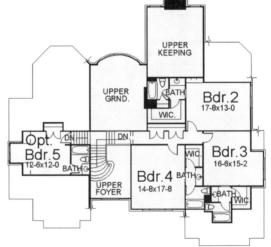

DESIGN HPT800128

First Floor: 2,670 square feet
Second Floor: 1,255 square feet
Total: 3,925 square feet

Width: 70'-6"
Depth: 66'-6"

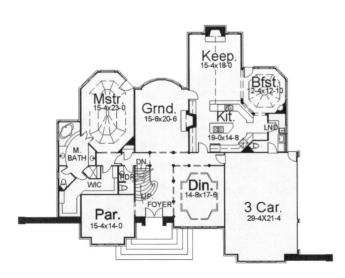

European extravagance, dazzled with chateau style, makes this enormous manor home the epitome of luxury and charm. A dramatic display of windows and a glorious arched entrance beautify the exterior. A dramatic staircase cascades into the foyer, which is flanked on either side by the formal dining room and parlor. The dining room is defined by its outlying columns. Straight ahead, the lofty two-story grand room is illuminated by a curved wall of windows at the rear. An enormous hearth warms the entire room and is flanked by built-in shelves. The cozy keeping room, warmed by a second fireplace, is open to both the casual bayed breakfast room and the gourmet island kitchen. The left wing of the main floor is almost entirely devoted to the master suite, which provides a large master bath with a whirlpool tub and a huge walk-in closet. Upstairs, all of the family bedrooms feature their own private baths.

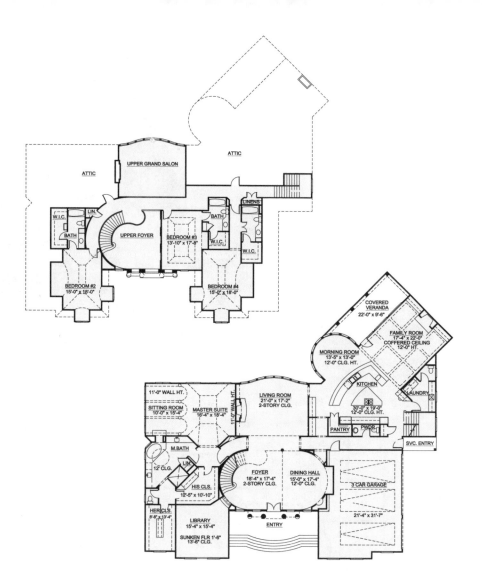

DESIGN HPT800129

First Floor: 3,652 square feet
Second Floor: 1,606 square feet
Total: 5,258 square feet

Width: 90'-0"
Depth: 85'-0"

Refined and detailed windows light up the facade of this home, as well as the interior. A royal estate is exactly what this home deserves to be called with its columned entry and subtle details. The two-story foyer is open to the dining hall which features an accentuated ceiling height. The living room is facing the backyard with a wall of windows to enjoy every last view. The wall of windows extends to the morning room which meets the covered veranda where views are also aplenty. The family room showcases a warming hearth where the family can meet and relax. The master suite is equipped with a sitting room and His and Hers closets. Three family rooms and attic space are located on the second floor.

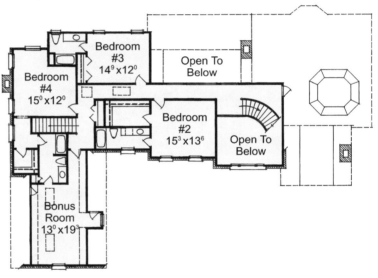

DESIGN HPT800130

First Floor: 2,871 square feet
Second Floor: 1,407 square feet
Total: 4,278 square feet

Bonus Space: 324 square feet
Width: 89'-3"
Depth: 60'-10"

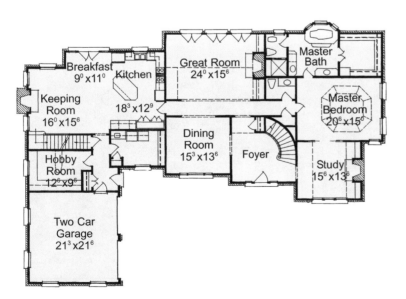

Brick details, casement windows and large expanses of glass add an Old World touch of glamour to this gracious two-story home. Sunlight streams into the two-story foyer, which is highlighted by the sweeping curves of the balustrade. For formal occasions, look to the spacious dining room, the inviting study and the vaulted great room. The kitchen, breakfast room and keeping room are designed for casual family living. The master suite provides a quiet retreat with access to the study through pocket doors. Luxury abounds in the spacious master bedroom and the sumptuous bath. Upstairs, three secondary bedrooms each have private baths. This home is designed with a basement foundation.

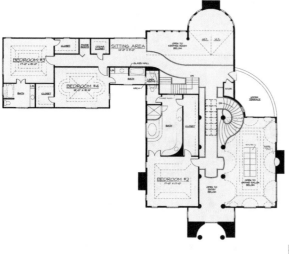

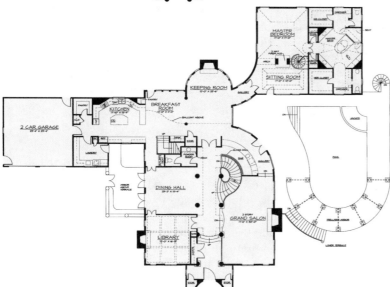

DESIGN HPT800131

First Floor: 4,209 square feet
Second Floor: 2,097 square feet
Total: 6,306 square feet

Width: 122'-0"
Depth: 98'-0"

Details, details—they make a significant difference in this posh estate home. The exterior reverberates with classic touches fit for any English country home. The interior is lavish in its use of space and decoration. The opposing library and grand salon capture an elegant era in entertaining—the dining room just beyond complements both. The keeping room, however, is surrounded in glass and connects to the breakfast room and island kitchen. In a completely separate wing, the master suite has its own sitting room, two cedar closets, His and Hers dressing areas and His and Hers closets. This suite accesses the pool/spa area which is highlighted by a trellised arbor. Upstairs bedrooms include one large enough to be used as a second master suite.

DESIGN HPT800074

First Floor: 4,865 square feet
Second Floor: 1,982 square feet
Total: 6,847 square feet

Width: 156'-2"
Depth: 85'-2"

This expansive home is a delight for owners and visitors alike. Meticulously placed windows add style and sophistication. Lofty ceilings create an elegant aura. The grand foyer features a two-story ceiling and showcases a circular staircase, which spirals upstairs onto the balcony leading to a game room, a study and two family bedrooms. Downstairs, the living and dining rooms are separated from the rest of the home with majestic columns and arches. The kitchen is connected to the breakfast and family room. The master suite is a fantastic retreat with a vaulted master bath and a bayed sitting area that has private access to the rear porch for those peaceful Sunday afternoons. An exercise room is also attached to the master bath with another private exit onto a separate rear porch.

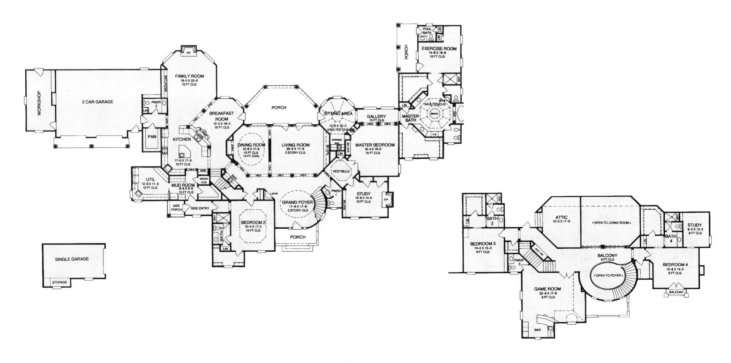

A Place in the Sun

Sparkling Sun Country and Mediterranean estates

Design HPT800162, see page 196

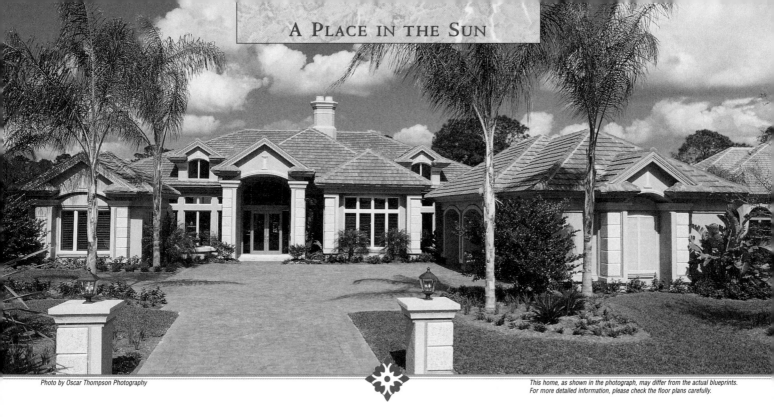

Photo by Oscar Thompson Photography

This home, as shown in the photograph, may differ from the actual blueprints. For more detailed information, please check the floor plans carefully.

Design HPT800132

Square Footage: 4,575

Width: 100'-0"

Depth: 126'-0"

This award-winning design is arranged in a flowing, open layout that uses richly detailed architectural elements to define the living and dining spaces. Comfortable living is guaranteed in the open leisure room, surrounded by walls of glass. An open skylight tops a secluded niche of the veranda, guarded by a privacy wall, creating an ideal place to enjoy meals outside. The leisure room opens to a morning nook and eating bar, both served by the kitchen. The spacious guest suite boasts a walk-in closet, full bath with a garden tub, and sliding glass door access to the veranda. The lavish master suite offers a private bath that features separate vanities.

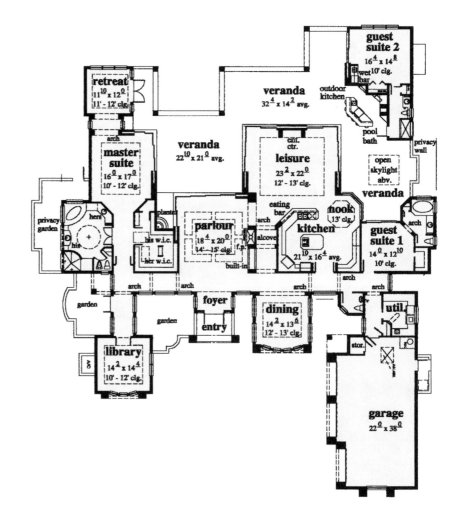

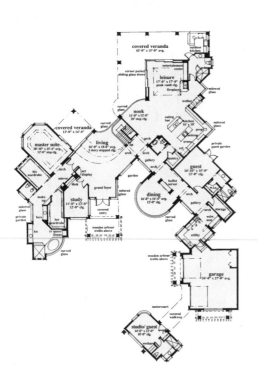

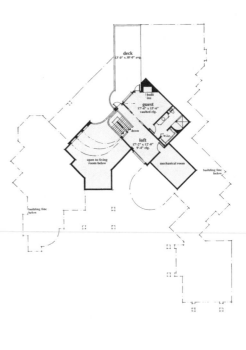

DESIGN HPT800133

First Floor: 4,470 square feet

Second Floor: 680 square feet

Total: 5,150 square feet

Studio/Guest Suite: 314 square feet

Width: 102'-0"

Depth: 131'-4"

The grand entry of this contemporary home gives way to an enticing interior. The living room features a two-story stepped ceiling and access to a covered veranda. The dining room, with a wall of curved glass, allows dramatic views and provides a buffet server for formal events. A leisure room includes a built-in entertainment center, wet bar and fireplace. Other special features include private gardens for the first-floor guest suite and master suite, a built-in desk in the study, two galleries, an art display niche and a rear veranda with an outdoor kitchen.

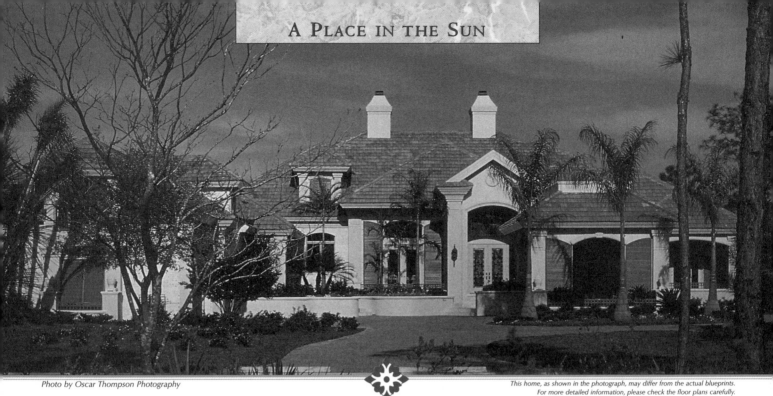

Photo by Oscar Thompson Photography

This home, as shown in the photograph, may differ from the actual blueprints. For more detailed information, please check the floor plans carefully.

DESIGN HPT800134

First Floor: 4,762 square feet
Second Floor: 775 square feet
Total: 5,537 square feet

Width: 100'-0"
Depth: 130'-0"

Stucco and shingles adorn the beautiful facade of this award-winning plan. A covered porte cochere shelters guests from the elements and provides a proper introduction to a home that will be easy to fall in love with. A fifteen-foot ceiling in the formal parlor creates a sense of grandeur, enhanced by open views. A butler's pantry connects the kitchen with the formal dining room. The master suite offers a private parlor that easily converts to a study. The private bath includes a walk-in shower, separate vanities and a glorious whirlpool tub with a garden view.

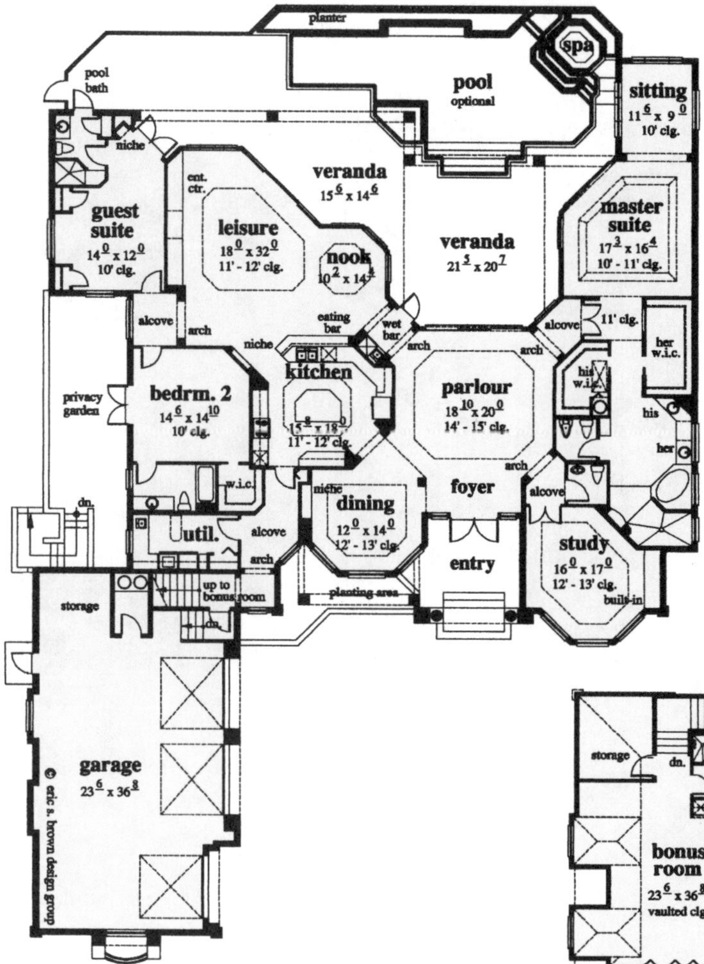

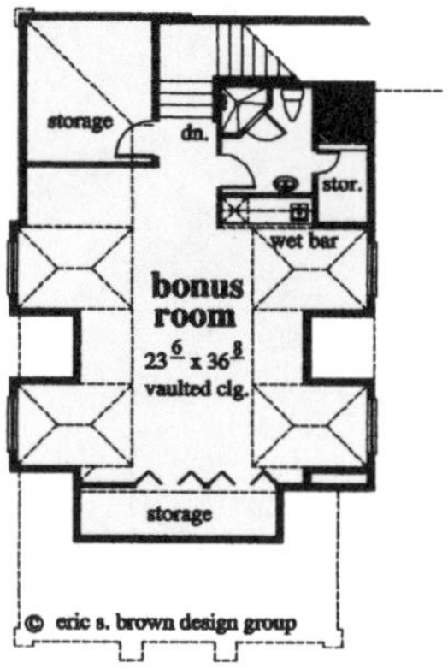

Floor plan labels:

planter
spa
pool bath
niche
pool optional
sitting 11'6 x 9'0 / 10' clg.
veranda 15'6 x 14'6
ent. ctr.
master suite 17'3 x 16'4 / 10' - 11' clg.
guest suite 14'0 x 12'0 / 10' clg.
leisure 18'0 x 32'0 / 11' - 12' clg.
nook 10'2 x 14'2
veranda 21'5 x 20'7
alcove
11' clg.
arch
eating bar
wet bar
alcove
her w.i.c.
privacy garden
bedrm. 2 14'6 x 14'10 / 10' clg.
kitchen
niche
15'2 x 18'2 / 11' - 12' clg.
parlour 18'10 x 20'0 / 14' - 15' clg.
his w.i.c.
his
her
w.i.c.
niche
dining 12'0 x 14'0 / 12' - 13' clg.
foyer
arch
alcove
dn.
util.
up to bonus room
alcove
arch
planting area
entry
study 16'0 x 17'2 / 12' - 13' clg. / built-in
storage
garage 23'6 x 36'8

© eric s. brown design group

storage
dn.
stor.
wet bar
bonus room 23'6 x 36'8 / vaulted clg.
storage

© eric s. brown design group

DESIGN HPT800135

Square Feet: 3,725
Bonus Space: 595 square feet
Width: 84'-3"
Depth: 115'-2"

This exotic Sun country dream home will brighten up any neighborhood. The pedimented entry is defined by strong columns and provides a very powerful look to this home. French doors lead the guests and homeowners into the parlor where a fabulous view of the rear veranda can be had. The well-laid out kitchen is conveniently located near the bayed formal dining room. The leisure room shares space with the breakfast nook. A guest suite has a private bath and French doors which open to the rear veranda. The lush master suite features many amenities including a sitting area and spacious His and Hers walk-in closets. The first floor also showcases a family bedroom and a study. A bonus room is found on the second floor.

Photo by Oscar Thompson Photography

This home, as shown in the photograph, may differ from the actual blueprints. For more detailed information, please check the floor plans carefully.

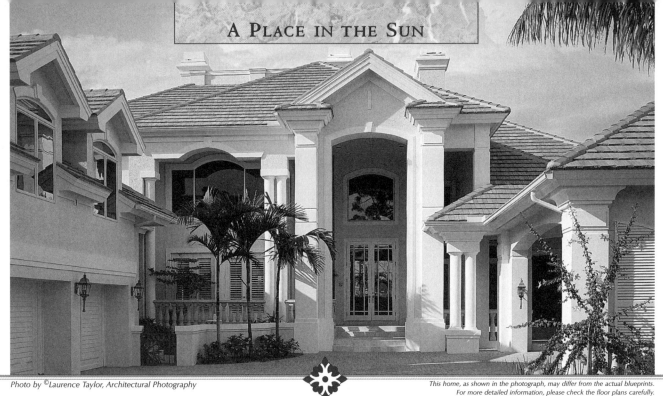

A PLACE IN THE SUN

Photo by ©Laurence Taylor, Architectural Photography

This home, as shown in the photograph, may differ from the actual blueprints. For more detailed information, please check the floor plans carefully.

DESIGN HPT800136

First Floor: 4,351 square feet
Second Floor: 1,200 square feet
Total: 5,551 square feet

Media/Loft Area: 454 square feet
Width: 114'-4"
Depth: 90'-2"

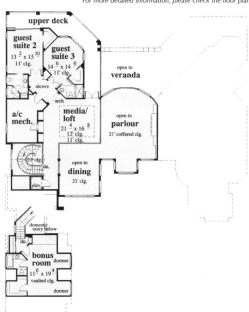

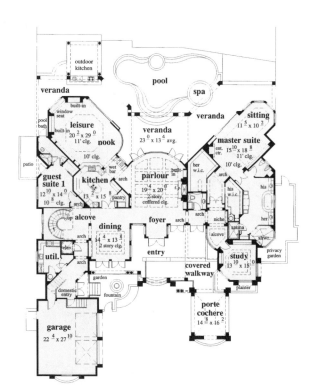

Graceful rooflines and a unique porte cochere complement a vaulted entry that suggests the grand, luxurious feel that fills this spectacular 21st-Century design. Quiet outdoor spaces add a natural touch, beginning with the covered walkway, private garden and fountain that surround the entry. Casual and formal rooms use the outdoor areas to extend the home's living space and take full advantage of the views provided through walls of glass. The heart of the home is a grand, two-story parlor with a coffered ceiling, a bay window and two sets of French doors leading to the veranda. The master suite features a built-in niche, glass doors to the veranda and a stunning sitting retreat that's brightened by a bay window. An alcove leads to a private study with a tray ceiling and built-ins.

DESIGN HPT800137

First Floor: 3,143 square feet
Second Floor: 1,348 square feet
Total: 4,491 square feet

Bonus Room: 368 square feet
Width: 89'-4"
Depth: 85'-9"

Double columns flank a raised loggia that leads to a beautiful two-story foyer. Flanking the elegant foyer is a formal dining room to the left while a den or study opens to the right. Straight ahead, under a balcony and defined by yet more pillars, is the spacious grand room. The master bedroom suite is lavish with its amenities, which include a bayed sitting area, direct access to the rear terrace, a walk-in closet and a sumptuous bath. The second floor is home to three family suites; Suite 4 enjoys its own full bath, while Suites 2 and 3 share a bath. Two small study areas, attic space and a bonus room for future expansion complete this plan.

Second Floor Plan

- SUITE 2 — 12'-6" x 14'-0"
- SUITE 3 — 12'-6" x 13'-0"
- SUITE 4 — 15'-0" x 14'-0"
- BATH
- OPEN TO GRAND RM.
- W.I.C.
- BALCONY
- W.I.C.
- BATH
- DN
- ATTIC
- DN
- SHELVES
- SHELVES
- DINING RM. VOLUME
- OPEN TO FOYER
- STUDY VOLUME
- BONUS ROOM — 16'-0" x 20'-6"
- ACCESS
- ACCESS
- ACCESS

First Floor Plan

- GATHERING ROOM — 14'-4" x 14'-4"
- MORNING ROOM — 13'-0" x 13'-6"
- COVERED TERRACE
- SITTING AREA
- WET BAR
- DESK
- KITCHEN — 19'-0" x 16'-0"
- PANT.
- GRAND ROOM — 22'-8" x 16'-0"
- MASTER SUITE — 15'-0" x 20'-0"
- MASTER BATH
- W.I.C.
- UP
- GALLERY
- UP
- PDR.
- DINING ROOM — 13'-6" x 14'-0"
- FOYER
- DEN/STUDY — 13'-6" x 14'-0"
- LAUNDRY
- LOGGIA
- COVERED PORCH
- GARAGE — 23'-0" x 29'-0"

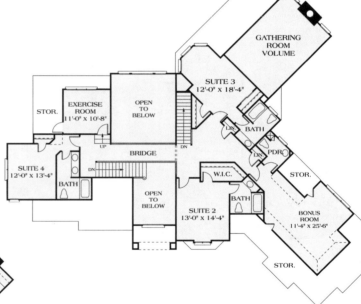

DESIGN HPT800138

First Floor: 2,733 square feet
Second Floor: 2,206 square feet
Total: 4,939 square feet

Bonus Room: 350 square feet
Width: 93'-7"
Depth: 78'-8"

Rounded windows and low, sloped arches accentuate the grandness of this home. A pedimented entrance leads to a two-story foyer which is flanked by a formal dining room and a study/living room. The angled kitchen looks into the sunny morning room and the two-story gathering room. The fireplace in the gathering room is a great view from the kitchen and morning room. Located on the first floor for privacy, the master bedroom suite is sure to please. It includes a huge walk-in closet, a separate shower and tub and a detailed ceiling. Three suites are upstairs and are complete with private baths. An exercise room, bonus room and powder room finish this floor.

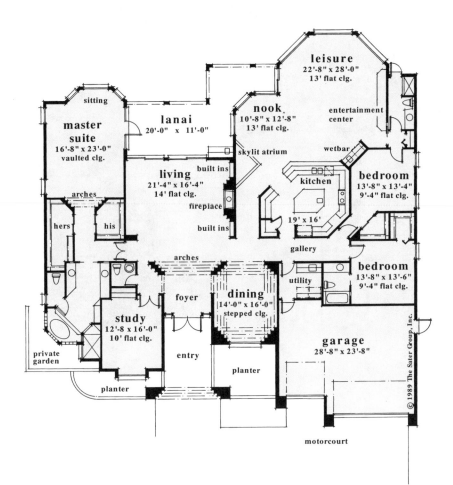

DESIGN HPT800139

Square Footage: 4,028

Width: 80'-0"
Depth: 82'-8"

The deep, rounded entry leads guests and homeowners into a lush, yet practical home. An interesting roofline adds charm to this home; custom details make it luxurious. The foyer and dining room feature stepped arches and ceiling treatments. The gallery leads past the indoor planter to the large kitchen, nook and leisure room. A built-in entertainment center and wet bar are nice touches to the breakfast nook and leisure rooms. The secondary bedrooms are full guest suites in their own right, but do not overshadow the master bedroom with its bayed sitting area and marvelous bath. A three-car garage connects to the main house via a utility room.

DESIGN HPT800140

First Floor: 2,551 square feet
Second Floor: 1,037 square feet
Total: 3,588 square feet

Width: 76'-0"
Depth: 90'-0"

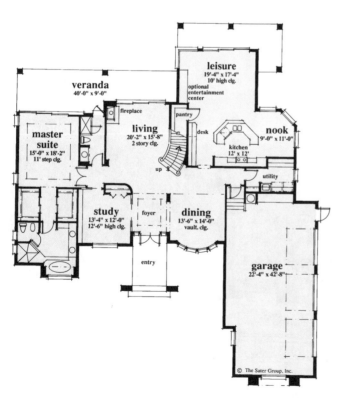

This beautiful home has many attributes, including a bowed dining room and a living room with a fireplace and outdoor access. For family gatherings, the kitchen remains open to the living areas. A study off the foyer will be much appreciated. A full bath leads to the outdoors—perfect for poolside. The master suite enjoys its own luxury bath with a whirlpool tub, dual lavatories, a compartmented toilet and bidet and a separate shower. Dual walk-in closets provide ample storage space. Upstairs, two bedrooms share a full bath. A loft with a wet bar accommodates playtime. A wrap-around deck is an added feature.

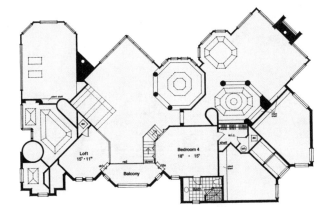

DESIGN HPT800141

First Floor: 3,770 square feet
Second Floor: 634 square feet
Total: 4,404 square feet

Width: 87'-0"
Depth: 97'-6"

This fresh and innovative design creates unbeatable ambiance. The breakfast nook and family room both open to a patio—a perfect arrangement for informal entertaining. The dining room is sure to please with elegant pillars separating it from the sunken living room. A media room delights both with its shape and convenience to the nearby kitchen—great for snack runs. A private garden surrounds the master bath and its spa tub and enormous walk-in closet. The master bedroom is enchanting with a fireplace and access to the outdoors. Additional family bedrooms come in a variety of different shapes and sizes; Bedroom 4 reigns over the second floor and features its own full bath.

DESIGN HPT800142

Square Footage: 4,187

Width: 84'-8"
Depth: 114'-0"

This contemporary masterpiece features many trendsetting details. The exterior lines are clean, but exciting. At the covered entry, a Palladian-style metal grill adds interest. Beyond the foyer, the living room opens up to the lanai through corner glass doors. The doors pocket into the wall, giving the feeling that the outdoors becomes one with the living area. The informal leisure area is perfect for family gatherings. Full guest suites and an exercise or hobby room are located in the guest wing. The master wing features a study with curved glass, a luxurious bath with His and Hers vanities, a large walk-in closet and a large sleeping area and sitting bay.

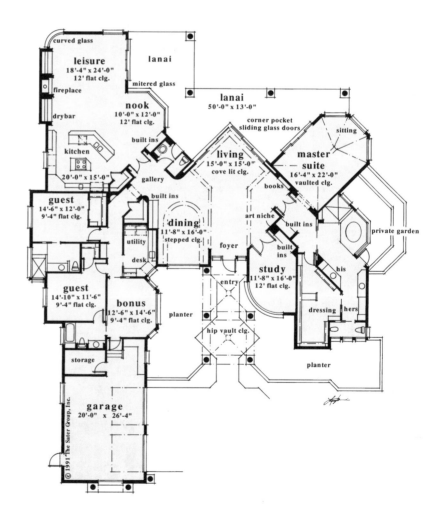

Square Footage: 3,866

Width: 120'-0"
Depth: 89'-0"

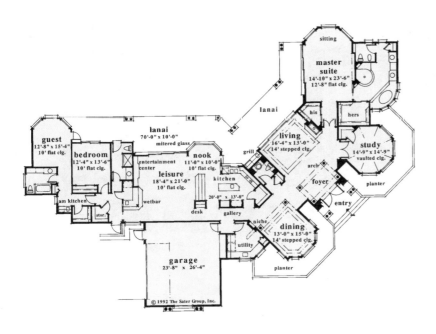

master
suite
14'-10" x 23'-6"
12'-8" flat clg.

sitting

his
hers

lanai

guest
12'-8" x 15'-4"
10' flat clg.

bedroom
12'-4" x 13'-6"
10' flat clg.

lanai
70'-0" x 10'-0"
mitered glass

entertainment
center

leisure
18'-4" x 21'-0"
10' flat clg.

nook
11'-0" x 10'-0"
10' flat clg.

living
16'-4" x 13'-0"
14' stepped clg.

grill

kitchen

arch

foyer

study
14'-9" x 14'-9"
vaulted clg.

planter

am kitchen

wetbar

desk

20'-0" x 13'-0"

gallery

niche

entry

stor.

garage
23'-8" x 26'-4"

utility

dining
13'-0" x 15'-0"
14' stepped clg.

planter

© 1992 The Sater Group, Inc.

This modern home adds a contemporary twist to the typical ranch-style plan. The turret study and bayed dining room add a sensuous look from the streetscape. The main living areas open up to the lanai and offer broad views to the rear through large expanses of glass and doors. The family kitchen, nook and leisure room focus on the lanai, the entertainment center and an ale bar. The guest suites have separate baths and also access the lanai. The master bath features a curved-glass shower, whirlpool tub, and private toilet and bidet room. Dual walk-in closets and an abundance of light further the appeal of this suite.

Design HPT800144

Square Footage: 3,556

Width: 85'-0"
Depth: 85'-0"

A beautifully curved portico provides a majestic entrance to this one-story home. French doors open into the foyer, to the left is a den/bedroom with a private bath, ideal for use as a guest suite and to the right of the foyer is a formal dining room with a magnificent volume ceiling. The exquisite master suite features a see-through fireplace and an exercise area with a wet bar. The family wing is geared for casual living with a powder room/patio bath, a huge island kitchen with a walk-in pantry, a glass-walled breakfast nook and a grand family room with a fireplace and media wall. Two family bedrooms share a private bath.

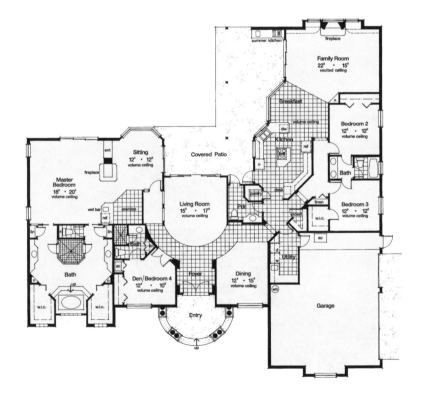

Deck

Bedroom 2
12' 6" x 17' 7"

ENT. CENTER

Clo   Clo   **Bath**   A.M. KITCHEN

DOWN

Bonus Space
24' 6" x 13' 10"

Clo

Bedroom 1
11' 4" x 21' 7"

Master Suite
14' 6" x 21' 0"

LITE COVE

Lanai
20' 4" x 7' 6"

Nook
12' 4" x 10' 8"

Lanai

BUILT-INS
BUILT-INS

Great Room
21' 4" x 16' 6"

ARCH

FIREPLACE

ARCH

Kitchen

His

Hers

BUILT-INS

CASED OPENING

GLASS SHOWER

Bath

Master Bath

BUILT-INS

FRAME DOWN ARCH

Study
11' 4" x 13' 9"

LITE COVE

Dining Room
11' 4" x 17' 6"

BARREL VAULT CEILING

ARCH

Garage
28' 6" x 22' 0"

UP

Pantry

Utility

WALK-IN SHOWER

OVERSIZE TUB

OPEN TO BELOW

DESIGN HPT800145

First Floor: 2,369 square feet
Second Floor: 1,230 square feet
Total: 3,599 square feet

Width: 89'-8"
Depth: 54'-0"

This Sun country home is dazzled with beautiful windows and a front turret. The spacious great room is enhanced by built-ins and a fireplace. An island workstation is thoughtfully placed in the kitchen for the gourmet. Through a graceful arch, the casual nook area accesses the rear and side lanais. The master suite is secluded for privacy and provides spacious His and Hers walk-in closets. The Master suite privately accesses the rear lanai through french doors. Bedroom 2 opens through double doors onto a sunny second-story deck. Bonus space is also located on the second floor, along with an A.M. kitchen.

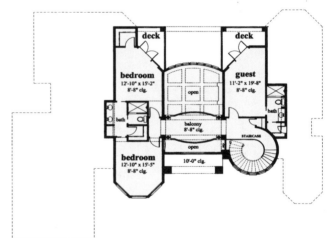

DESIGN HPT800146

First Floor: 2,841 square feet

Second Floor: 1,052 square feet

Total: 3,893 square feet

Width: 85'-0"
Depth: 76'-8"

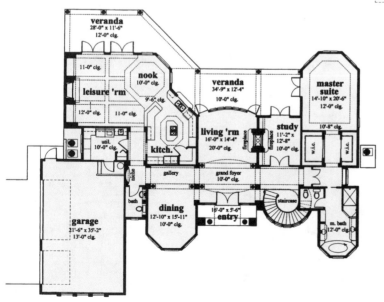

Elegant living is assured with this luxurious plan. A turret, two-story bay windows and plenty of arched glass impart a graceful style to the exterior, while rich amenities inside furnish contentment. A grand foyer decked with columns introduces the living room with a curve of glass windows viewing the rear gardens. A through-fireplace is shared by the study and living room. The master suite enjoys a tray ceiling, two walk-in closets, a separate shower and garden tub set in a bay window. Informal entertainment will be a breeze with a rich leisure room adjoining the kitchen and breakfast nook and opening to a rear veranda. At the top of a lavish curving staircase are two family bedrooms sharing a full bath and a guest suite with a private deck.

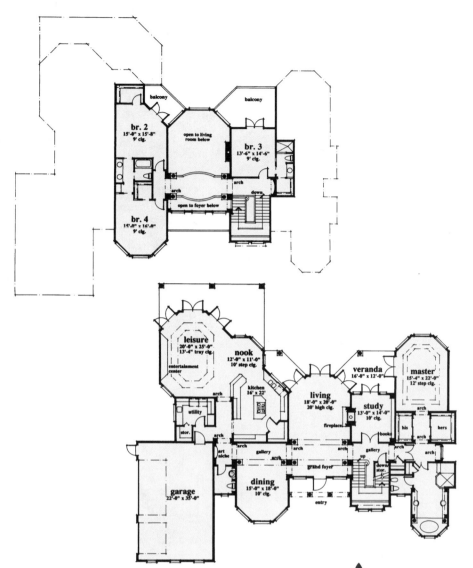

DESIGN HPT800147

First Floor: 3,546 square feet
Second Floor: 1,213 square feet
Total: 4,759 square feet

Width: 95'-4"
Depth: 83'-0"

This grand traditional home offers an elegant, welcoming residence for the homeowner with luxury in mind. The grand foyer opens onto a wonderful display of casual and formal living areas. Beyond the foyer, the spacious living room provides views of the rear grounds and opens to the veranda and rear yard through three pairs of French doors. An arched gallery hall leads past the formal dining room to the family areas. Here, an ample gourmet kitchen easily serves the nook and the leisure room. The homeowner's wing includes a study or home office. Upstairs, each of three secondary bedrooms features a walk-in closet, and two bedrooms offer a private balcony. Please specify basement or slab foundation when ordering.

DESIGN HPT800148

First Floor: 3,027 square feet

Second Floor: 1,079 square feet

Total: 4,106 square feet

Width: 87'-4"
Depth: 80'-4"

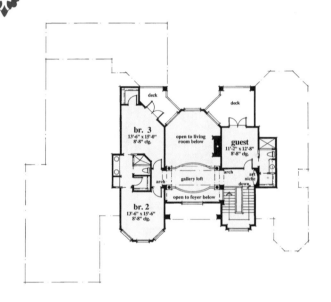

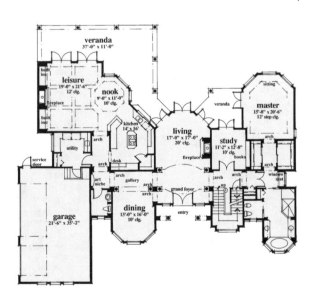

The inside of this design is just as majestic as the outside. The grand foyer is dramatically highlighted by pillars and opens to a two-story living room with a fireplace, magnificent views and access to both rear verandas. An octagonal tower will make dining in the formal dining room a memorable experience. Pillared arches lead traffic to the casual family area, which includes a well-designed kitchen, a sunny nook and a leisure room with a fireplace and outdoor access. The master wing includes a separate study and an elegant private bath with two walk-in closets, separate basins and a corner tub that will call to you after a long day. The second level features a guest suite with its own bath and deck, two family bedrooms (Bedroom 3 also has its own deck) and a gallery loft with views to the living room below. Please specify basement or slab foundation when ordering.

Turrets top the foyer and dining room to make this home a Sun country classic. Intricate detailing envelops every inch of this well-crafted home—from the shutters to the door design. High ceilings are found throughout this amazing home; both the foyer and parlor have two-story ceilings. The leisure room is near the breakfast nook and the kitchen for great servability. A pantry is located right outside the formal dining room for those nights of entertaining. A study is located at the rear of the home complete with windows and private French doors leading to the rear veranda. Two guest suites and a parlor are also found on the first level. A lush master suite is located on the second level, complete with His and Hers closets, whirlpool bath, French doors accessing the rear deck and plenty of window light. A media room can also be found on the second level.

DESIGN HPT800149

First Floor: 4,233 square feet
Second Floor: 781 square feet
Total: 5,014 square feet

Loft/Media Room: 373 square feet
Width: 103'-10"
Depth: 102'-8"

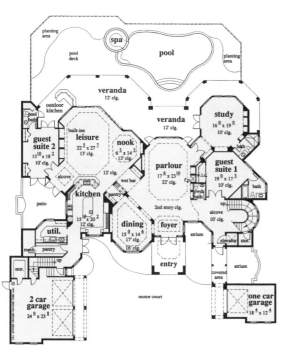

Design HPT800150

First Floor: 2,899 square feet
Second Floor: 1,472 square feet
Total: 4,371 square feet

Width: 69'-4"
Depth: 76'-8"

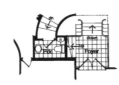

Finished with French country adornments, this estate home is comfortable in just about any setting. Main living areas are sunken down just a bit from the entry foyer, providing them with soaring ceilings and sweeping views. Just to the left of the living room and around the corner are another series of stairs leading to an optional secluded powder room. The family room features a focal fireplace. A columned entry gains access to the master suite where separate sitting and sleeping areas are defined by a three-sided fireplace. There are three bedrooms upstairs; one has a private bath. The media room on this level is sunken a few steps and has storage space. Look for the decks on the second level.

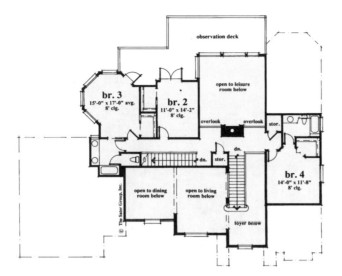

observation deck

br. 3
15'-0" x 17'-0" avg.
8' clg.

br. 2
11'-0" x 14'-2"
8' clg.

open to leisure
room below

overlook   overlook   stor.

dn.

dn.   dn.   stor.

br. 4
14'-0" x 11'-8"
8' clg.

open to dining
room below   open to living
room below

foyer below

© The Sater Group, Inc.

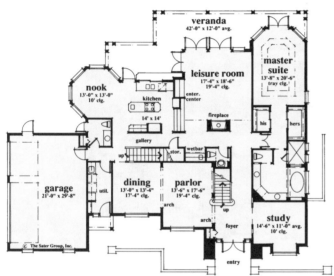

veranda
42'-0" x 12'-0" avg.

nook
13'-0" x 13'-0"
10' clg.

leisure room
17'-4" x 18'-6"
19'-4" clg.

master
suite
13'-8" x 20'-6"
tray clg.

kitchen
14' x 14'

enter.
center

his   hers

fireplace

gallery

wetbar

garage
21'-0" x 29'-8"

util.

up   stor.

dining
13'-0" x 13'-4"
17'-4" clg.

parlor
13'-6" x 17'-6"
19'-4" clg.

arch

arch

foyer

up

study
14'-6" x 11'-0" avg.
10' clg.

entry

© The Sater Group, Inc.

DESIGN HPT800151

First Floor: 2,638 square feet
Second Floor: 1,032 square feet
Total: 3,670 square feet

Width: 80'-4"
Depth: 65'-4"

Unique window treatments, glass walls and French doors provide panoramic views from every room in this sophisticated home. Natural light fills a two-story foyer that opens to a study to the right and a formal parlor and dining room to the left. The leisure room is located to the rear of the plan and provides access to the veranda via three sets of French doors, creating a perfect setting for casual gatherings. The kitchen features an island cooktop and easily serves the sunny breakfast nook. The master suite is a private getaway that invites relaxation. His and Hers walk-in closets and a luxurious bath are sure to please. The second floor contains three family bedrooms—all with walk-in closets—and two full baths.

Design HPT800152

First Floor: 4,760 square feet

Second Floor: 1,552 square feet

Total: 6,312 square feet

Width: 98'-0"

Depth: 103'-8"

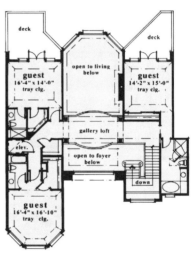

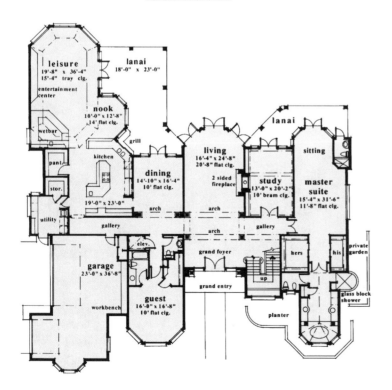

As beautiful from the rear as from the front, this home features a spectacular blend of arch-top windows, French doors and balusters. Dramatic two-story ceilings and tray details add custom spaciousness. An impressive, informal leisure room has a sixteen-foot tray ceiling, an entertainment center and a grand ale bar. The large gourmet kitchen is well appointed and easily serves the nook and formal dining room. The master suite has a large bedroom and a bayed sitting area. His and Hers vanities and walk-in closets and a curved, glass-block shower are highlights in the bath. The staircase leads to the deluxe secondary guest suites, two of which have observation decks to the rear and each with their own full baths.

DESIGN HPT800153

First Floor: 2,470 square feet
Second Floor: 1,360 square feet
Total: 3,830 square feet

Width: 77'-4"
Depth: 59'-8"

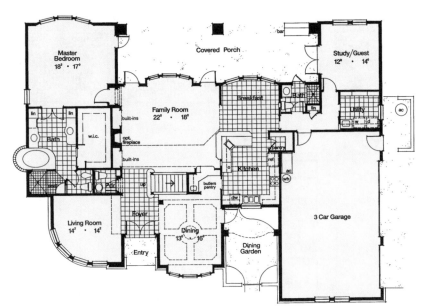

This design embraces the outdoors so well, it's almost difficult to distinguish where inside living areas end and outdoor spaces begin. Notice, for instance, the delightful dining garden, snuggled in between the formal dining room and the garage. Above it is a balcony adorning Bedroom 5. The family room has a curved glass view of the covered porch to the rear of the home; the living room echoes this option to the front. Even the dining room and master bedroom utilize curved glass accents. There is no lack of room in this design, either. Five bedrooms include a gallant master suite. Plus, the cozy study can become a guest bedroom as it is near a full bath. The second-level loft is a great place for quiet study or reading.

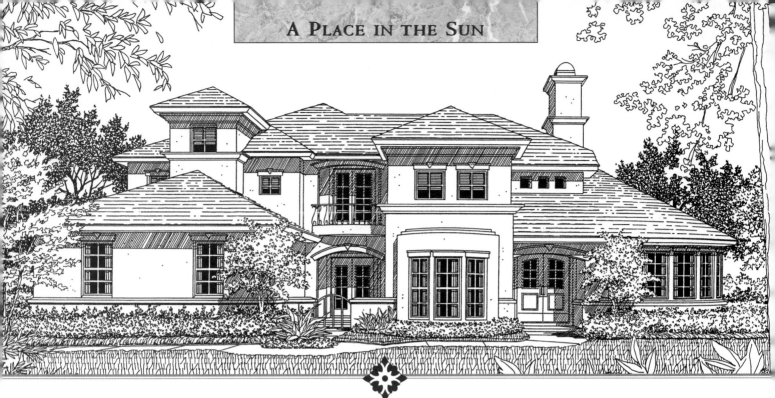

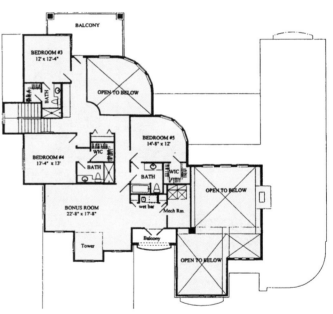

DESIGN HPT800154

First Floor: 3,566 square feet

Second Floor: 1,196 square feet

Total: 4,762 square feet

Bonus Space: 479 square feet

Width: 85'-0"

Depth: 81'-4"

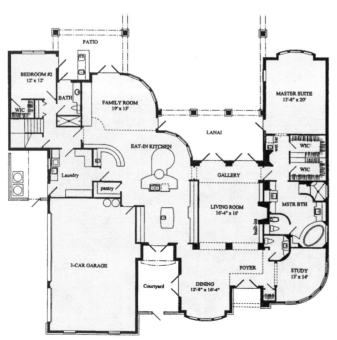

Blend the best elements of Spanish Colonial and contemporary design, and the result is an estate such as this. There are two ways to enter: through the main entry that separates the study and the dining room, or through the courtyard entry that leads directly into the eat-in kitchen. The living room is assigned columns and has a lovely gallery leading to the rear lanai. The family room is snug. It is a gateway to a private patio with a summer kitchen. A guest bedroom and master suite complete this level. The second floor holds three family bedrooms and access to two balconies (one with a nearby wet bar). Bonus space features a light-filled tower—make this hobby or study space.

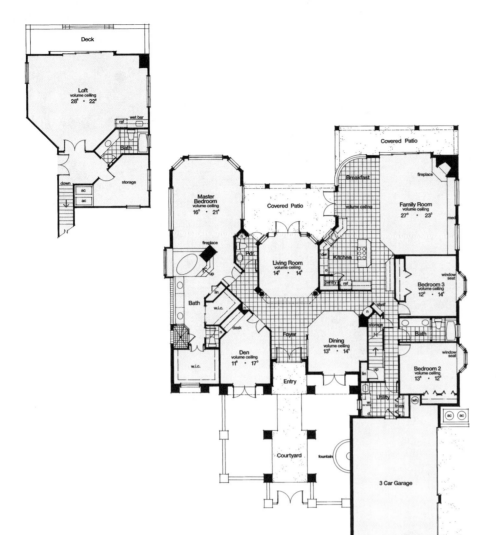

DESIGN HPT800155

First Floor: 3,395 square feet
Second Floor: 757 square feet
Total: 4,152 square feet

Width: 71'-0"
Depth: 100'-8"

Old World Mediterranean flavor spills over and combines with classic contemporary lines through the courtyard and at the double door entry to this three-bedroom home. The formal living room is defined by columns and a glass wall that looks out over the rear patio. The formal dining room offers access to the front courtyard with French doors. A den/library also has French doors to the courtyard and accesses the pool bath for the occasional guest. Double doors bring you into the world of the master suite and sumptuous luxury. A lavish bath features a soaking tub, glass enclosed shower and His and Hers walk-in closets. Two large family bedrooms, both with bay windows, share a full bath. A spectacular loft awaits upstairs to accommodate a home theater, game room or bedroom areas.

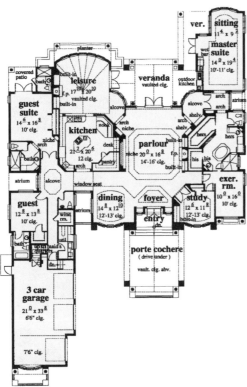

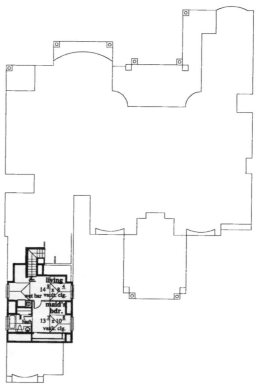

DESIGN HPT800156

First Floor: 4,585 square feet

Second Floor: 525 square feet

Total: 5,110 square feet

Width: 84'-0"
Depth: 129'-8"

Straightforward lines, a wraparound veranda, high-pitched rooflines and a host of atriums blur the separation between the living areas of this stunning stucco home and the natural world that surrounds it. The dining room faces the front garden. A beautiful bowed window and tray ceiling help to define this formal room. The leisure room provides access to the rear veranda. The kitchen boasts an eat-in table in the morning nook. The master suite is a truly opulent retreat—the bedroom provides a wet bar, sitting area, tray ceiling, bay window and doors to the veranda and outdoor kitchen.

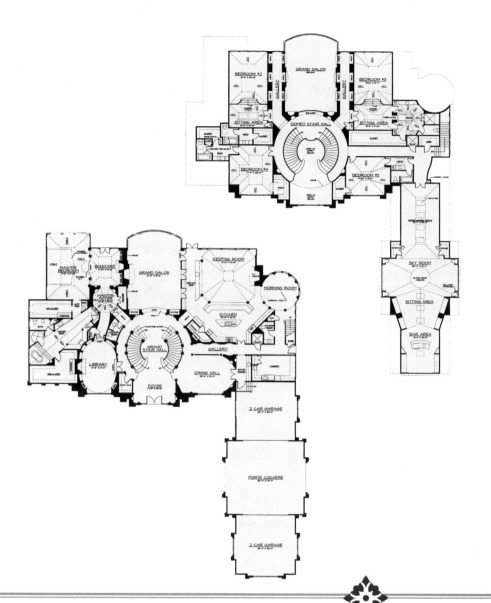

DESIGN HPT800157

First Floor: 6,198 square feet
Second Floor: 3,547 square feet
Total: 9,745 square feet

Bonus Space: 1,584 square feet
Width: 106'-0"
Depth: 77'-0"

Awe-inspiring architecture made possible this formidable estate. For true indulgence, it is unsurpassed. While it would take volumes to explain in detail all of the delights of this home, some of its most notable features include a spectacular grand stair hall, an oval library, a glass-enclosed morning room, an immense keeping room and a two-story grand salon. The master suite is all you could wish for. It features a separate boudoir, His and Hers closets with built-in dressers, and a uniquely shaped bath. Upstairs family bedrooms include two with private sitting rooms. An interesting use of space—and a delightful addition—the skyroom makes use of a glass dome to light entertainment space and a bar area. Double garages flank a porte cochere parking area.

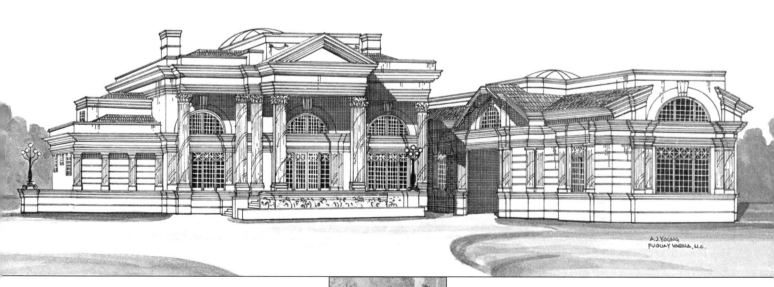

DESIGN HPT800158

First Floor: 3,264 square feet
Second Floor: 1,671 square feet
Total: 4,935 square feet

Width: 96'-10"
Depth: 65'-1"

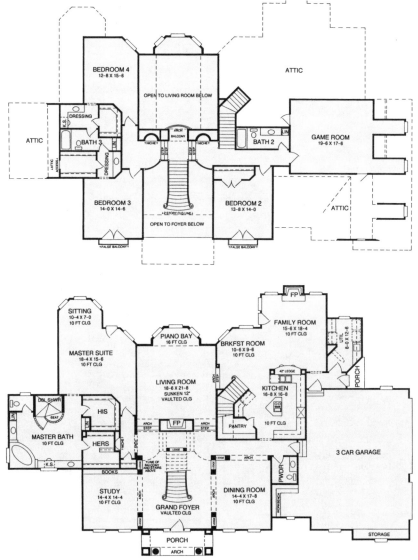

An impressive entry, multi-pane windows and mock balconies combine to give this facade an elegance of which to be proud. The grand foyer showcases a stunning staircase and is flanked by a formal dining room to the right and a cozy study to the left. The elegant sunken living room is graced by a fireplace, a wondrous piano bay, and a vaulted ceiling. The openness of the sunny breakfast room and the family room make casual entertaining a breeze. Located on the first floor for privacy, the master bedroom suite is lavish with its luxuries. A bayed sitting area encourages early morning repose, while the bath revels in pampering you. Upstairs, three bedrooms share two full baths and have access to a large game room over the three-car garage. Please specify crawlspace or slab foundation when ordering.

BR. 3
12/2 X 13/8
(9' CLG.)

LIVING RM
BELOW

ATTIC

BR. 2
12/8 X 18/0
(9' CLG.)

OPEN TO FOYER

BR. 4
14/0 X 12/2
(9' CLG.)

LINEN

DN.

First Floor: 3,020 square feet
Second Floor: 1,060 square feet
Total: 4,080 square feet

Width: 112'-0"
Depth: 75'-8"

MASTER
17/4 X 15/6
(10' CLG.)

LIVING
(2) STORY
16/0 X 17/6

FAMILY
17/6 X 18/0
(10' CLG.)

NOOK
10/0 X 13/0
(10' CLG.)

PLANTER

PLANTER

DEN
14/0 X 14/10
(10' CLG.)

2 STORY
FOYER

UP

DINING
18/0 X 13/10
(10' CLG.)

GARAGE
25/0 X 33/0

NICHE

NICHE

This beloved Sun country home is wrapped in European delight from its window detailing to its low, sloping rooflines. A keystone and lintel add decorative style to the French-door entryway. The two-story foyer is flanked by the den and dining room. A fireplace is featured in the dining room and is sure to light up any meal. Another fireplace can be enjoyed while relaxing in the living room. Yet another fireplace is found in the most comforting room in the house, the family room. A breakfast nook also shares the warmth of the family-room fireplace. A snack-bar kitchen conveniently serves both the breakfast nook and family room. Three family bedrooms and attic space are found on the second floor.

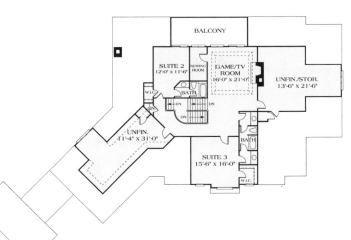

DESIGN HPT800160

First Floor: 3,562 square feet
Second Floor: 1,366 square feet
Total: 4,928 square feet

Bonus Space: 957 square feet
Width: 134'-8"
Depth: 89'-8"

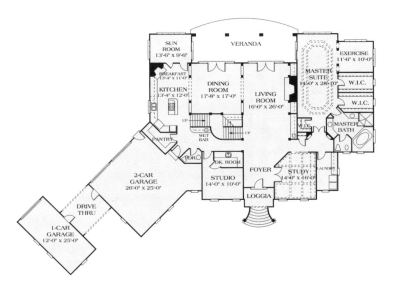

Making a grand entrance is almost required with this fine two-story stucco home. The elegant loggia leads to the foyer where a beam-ceilinged study waits on the right. Directly ahead is a wonderfully large living room, complete with a warming fireplace, built-ins and access to the rear veranda. A spacious formal dining room also offers access to the veranda and is easily serviced by the large island kitchen. Note the studio at the front of the home, with a built-in darkroom. The deluxe master suite is designed to pamper. Upstairs, two suites offer private baths and walk-in closets. A game/TV room is enhanced by a third fireplace and sits adjacent to a sewing room. There are two large unfinished rooms completing this floor.

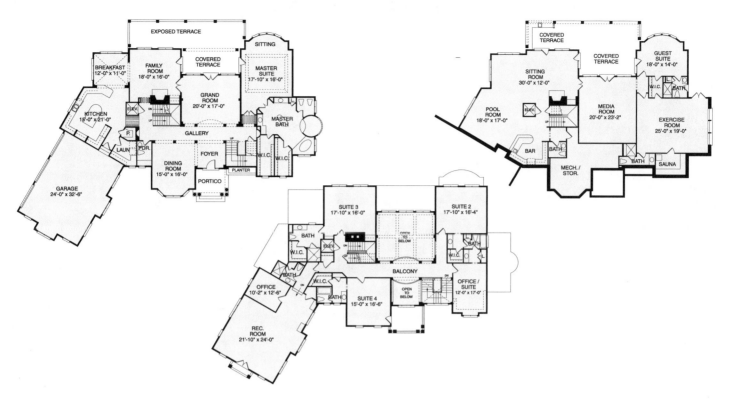

DESIGN HPT800161

First Floor: 3,300 square feet

Second Floor: 1,973 square feet

Total: 5,273 square feet

Finished Basement: 2,870 square feet

Width: 107'-10"

Depth: 75'-7"

Expansive windows surround this Sun country home and light drowns the interior, making for the perfect living environment. Great formal entertaining and family lounging areas are located on the first floor, including a columned dining room and grand room. The fireplace-warmed family room is adjacent to the cozy breakfast nook and spacious kitchen. The master suite is also located on the first floor. A sitting room, dual vanities and walk-in closets make this suite a pure delight. On the second floor, three suites are located, as well as two offices and a grand recreation room. The basement floor consists of a family sitting room, media room and exercise room, as well as a guest suite and pool room.

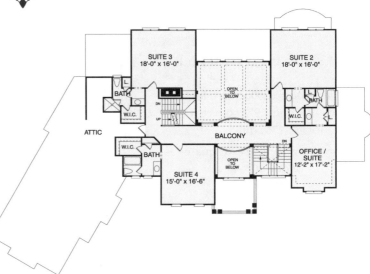

DESIGN HPT800162

First Floor: 3,300 square feet

Second Floor: 1,974 square feet

Total: 5,274 square feet

Finished Basement: 1,896 square feet

Storage Area: 1,273 square feet

Width: 108'-2"

Depth: 74'-7"

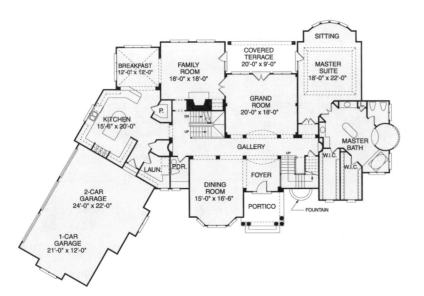

Here is a Sun country classic complete with grand windows, columned entry and a balcony overhead. Windows wrap the home with sunshine. The bright floor plan includes a grand room—perfect for formal occasions—a family room featuring a fireplace—ideal for quality family time—and an expansive kitchen complete with a pantry and island. The master suite includes a sitting room with a ribbon of windows, two walk-in closets, dual vanities and private access to the rear covered terrace. The second floor showcases three suites, each with their own bath, and an office.

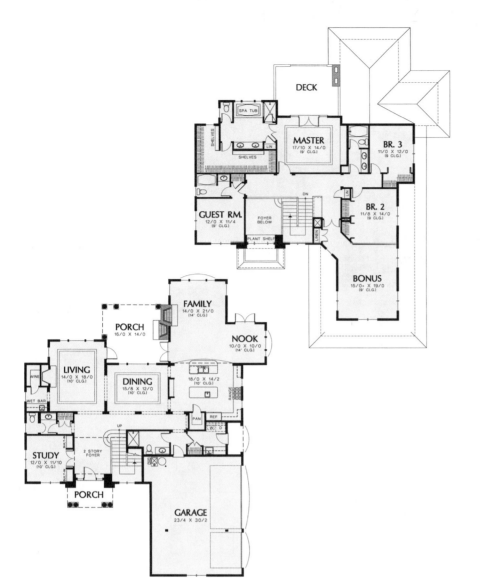

DECK

SPA TUB

SHELVES

SHELVES

MASTER
17/10 X 14/0
(9' CLG.)

BR. 3
11/0 X 12/0
(9' CLG.)

GUEST RM.
12/0 X 11/4
(9' CLG.)

FOYER
BELOW

DN

BR. 2
11/8 X 14/0
(9' CLG.)

LINEN

PLANT SHELF

BONUS
15/0+ X 19/0
(9' CLG.)

FAMILY
14/0 X 21/0
(14' CLG.)

PORCH
16/0 X 14/0

NOOK
10/0 X 10/0
(14' CLG.)

LIVING
14/0 X 18/0
(10' CLG.)

DINING
15/8 X 12/0
(10' CLG.)

18/0 X 14/2
(10' CLG.)

WINE

RANGE

WET BAR

PAN   REF

UP

W   D

STUDY
12/0 X 11/10
(10' CLG.)

2 STORY
FOYER

PORCH

GARAGE
23/4 X 30/2

DESIGN HPT800163

First Floor: 2,035 square feet
Second Floor: 1,543 square feet
Total: 3,578 square feet

Bonus Room: 366 square feet
Width: 62'-0"
Depth: 76'-0"

Twin-set columns usher one into the two-story foyer of this fine home. A quiet study to the left would make a good home office. Entertaining will truly be pleasant, with a formal living room—complete with fireplace—a formal dining room and a spacious family room all opening onto a large covered porch—perfect for catching the ocean breezes. Note the fireplace in the family room and another on the porch. The kitchen will please the gourmet of the family with its abundance of amenities. Upstairs, two family bedrooms share a full bath and access to a large bonus room. A guest room is nicely separate from the family rooms and offers a private bath. The lavish master suite is designed to pamper with a private deck, a huge walk-in closet and a deluxe bath.

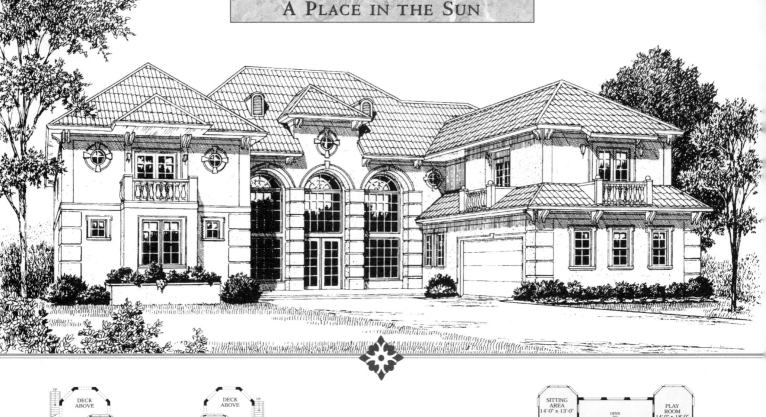

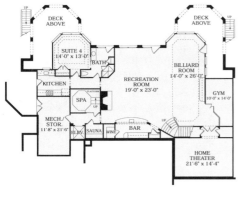

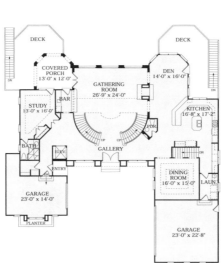

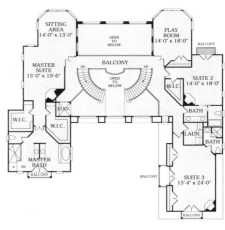

DESIGN HPT800164

First Floor: 2,710 square feet

Second Floor: 2,784 square feet

Total: 5,494 square feet

Finished Basement: 2,574 square feet

Width: 79'-4"

Depth: 76'-8"

This Sun country stucco delight is wrapped in windows that lend the entire home warmth and brightness. Two-story clerestory windows are perfect for homeowners who appreciate the wide-open feel. French doors lead to the gallery and dual staircases. The gathering room is straight back, glowing with the backyard, as there are three two-story windows. The covered porch and den are on either side of the gathering room with decks just off both of them. The master suite is located on the second floor, complete with two walk-in closets, dual vanities, and a comfortable sitting area. A playroom and two suites are also found on the second floor. The basement opens to the backyard and features a recreation room, billiard room and a gym to name a few amenities.

Second floor plan:
ATTIC STOR.

BATH

OPEN TO BELOW

BATH

SUITE 4
15'-0" x 16'-8"

BALCONY

SUITE 3
13'-6" x 13'-0"

OPEN TO BELOW

LEDGE

SUITE 2
13'-4" x 13'-0"

W.I.C.   W.I.C.

ATTIC STOR.

DESIGN HPT800165

First Floor: 2,538 square feet

Second Floor: 1,171 square feet

Total: 3,709 square feet

Finished Basement: 1,784 square feet

Width: 67'-7"

Depth: 85'-1"

First floor plan:
MASTER SUITE
13'-4" x 19'-6"

DECK

LAKE DINING
9'-6" x 13'-0"

LAKE GATHERING
17'-0" x 18'-6"

LAKE LIVING
19'-10" x 15'-0"

KITCHEN
19'-6" x 16'-8"

W.I.C.

GALLERY

MASTER BATH

FOYER

DINING ROOM
13'-4" x 12'-4"

PDR.

P.

LAUNDRY

PORTICO

2-CAR GARAGE
23'-0" x 20'-0"

1-CAR GARAGE
20'-0" x 12'-0"

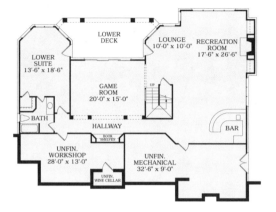

Basement plan:
LOWER DECK

LOUNGE
10'-0" x 10'-0"

RECREATION ROOM
17'-6" x 26'-6"

LOWER SUITE
13'-6" x 18'-6"

GAME ROOM
20'-0" x 15'-0"

UP

BATH

HALLWAY

BAR

UNFIN. WORKSHOP
28'-0" x 13'-0"

BOOK SHELVES

UNFIN. MECHANICAL
32'-6" x 9'-0"

UNFIN. WINE CELLAR

A classic portico gives entry to this charming Mediterranean estate, which offers rooms that fit well with today's lifestyles. The master suite, with a private bath and access to the deck, dominates the left side of the first floor; casual living areas, such as the kitchen and lake gathering and dining rooms, reside to the right of the plan. A gallery spans the length of the lake living room. Upstairs, three suites—one with a private bath—share a balcony that overlooks the living room.

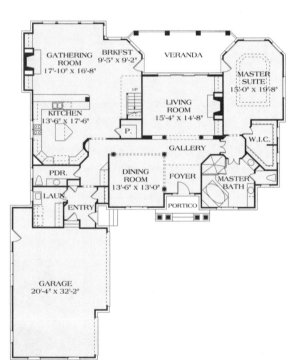

GATHERING ROOM 17'-10" x 16'-8"

BRKFST 9'-5" x 9'-2"

VERANDA

MASTER SUITE 15'-0" x 19'-8"

KITCHEN 13'-6" x 17'-6"

UP

LIVING ROOM 15'-4" x 14'-8"

P.

W.I.C.

PDR.

GALLERY

DINING ROOM 13'-6" x 13'-0"

FOYER

MASTER BATH

LAUN.

ENTRY

PORTICO

GARAGE 20'-4" x 32'-2"

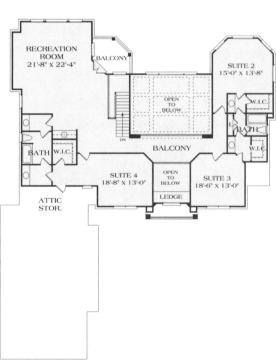

RECREATION ROOM 21'-8" x 22'-4"

BALCONY

SUITE 2 15'-0" x 13'-8"

OPEN TO BELOW

W.I.C.

DN

BATH

W.I.C.

BATH

BALCONY

W.I.C.

ATTIC STOR.

SUITE 4 18'-8" x 13'-0"

OPEN TO BELOW

LEDGE

SUITE 3 18'-6" x 13'-0"

DESIGN HPT800166

First Floor: 2,569 square feet
Second Floor: 1,890 square feet
Total: 4,459 square feet

Width: 69'-1"
Depth: 85'-1"

This majestic two-story home frames the columned entryway with a balcony above. The expansive windows add a bit of mystery to the overall sophistication of this home. The formal dining room is defined by columns, as an arched entry leads to the living room where a fireplace warms the home. The breakfast nook shares space with the gathering room—which also features a fireplace. Views from the rear veranda can be enjoyed throughout the home. The kitchen offers plenty of preparation space with an island in the middle. The master suite is complete with a lavish master bath and a spacious closet. A great recreation room is located on the second level for the whole family. Three suites are also found on the second level.

Bedroom 3
12⁴ · 13⁰

Bath 3

Bedroom 4
12⁴ · 13⁰

W.I.C.

W.I.C.

Loft

Bath 2

W.I.C.

down

Foyer Below

Bedroom 2
12⁴ · 11⁴

False Balcony

Bonus Room
33⁴ · 12⁰

down

Master Bedroom
15⁴ · 20⁰
Tray Clg.

3 Car Garage
32⁴ · 19⁰

Pool Bath

W.I.C.

Laundry

medis wal

Master Bath

W.I.C.

Covered Patio

Family Room
17⁴ · 22⁰
Vaulted Clg.

Living
16⁴ · 13⁰

Nook

W.I.C.

Den
15⁴ · 11⁴

Kitchen

range

down

Garden

Mech.

Butler's Pantry

pantry

Pwdr.

Wine

Foyer

Dining
12⁴ · 13⁰

Entry

down

DESIGN HPT800167

First Floor: 3,079 square feet
Second Floor: 1,015 square feet
Total: 4,094 square feet

Bonus Room: 425 square feet
Width: 77'-4"
Depth: 82'-8"

Imagine yourself in the south of France with this French Provincial home. Inside, head straight for the beam-ceiling living room, which looks out to the covered porch. The breakfast room, kitchen and family room are all connected by the kitchen's island/snack bar. Enjoy formal dining at the front of the house, with a tray ceiling overhead. The master suite features a wall of windows, two walk-in closets and a luxurious private bath. Three bedrooms occupy the second level; two share a full bath, while the third includes a private bath. Other amenities include a den—which has a walk-in closet and French doors leading to a private garden—a wine cellar and a powder room off the garage for swimming parties.

Design HPT800168

Main Level: 2,959 square feet
Upper Level: 1,055 square feet
Lower Level: 1,270 square feet
Total: 5,284 square feet

Width: 110'-4"
Depth: 72'-5"

Designed for a sloping lot, this fantastic Mediterranean home features all the views to the rear, making it the perfect home for an ocean, lake or golf-course view. Inside, the great room features a rear wall of windows. The breakfast room, kitchen, dining room and master suite also feature rear views. A three-level series of porches is located on the back for outdoor relaxing. Two bedroom suites are found upstairs, each with a private bath and a porch. The basement of this home features another bedroom suite and a large game room. An expandable area can be used as an office or Bedroom 5. Please specify basement or slab foundation when ordering.

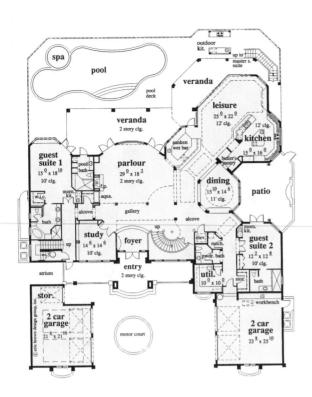

First floor plan labels:
spa, pool, outdoor kit., up to master s. suite, veranda, pool deck, veranda 2 story clg., leisure 25⁰ x 22⁰ 12' clg., kitchen 15⁰ x 16⁰, sunken wet bar, butler's pantry, mom. kit., guest suite 1 15⁰ x 18¹⁰ 10' clg., pool bath, parlour 29⁰ x 18² 2 story clg., f.p., dining 15¹⁰ x 14⁶ 11' clg., patio, w.i.c., mom. kit., aqua., alcove, gallery, alcove, bath, up, study 14⁶ x 14⁶ 10' clg., foyer, up, +, elev., mech., mom. kit., guest suite 2 12² x 12⁸ 10' clg., atrium, entry 2 story clg., pwdr. bath, util. 10⁰ x 10², stor., bath, stor., 2 car garage 21⁸ x 21, motor court, workbench, 2 car garage 23⁸ x 25¹⁰

© eric brown design group, inc.

Second floor plan labels:
deck, office 10' clg., open to veranda, master suite 16⁸ x 15⁸ 10' clg., guest suite 3 15⁴ x 17⁶ 10' clg., deck, sitting 12⁰ x 14⁰ 10' clg., m. bath, shwr., steam, w.i.c., open to parlour 24⁴ clg., mom. kit., hers w.i.c., bath, loft 12' clg., bridge, loft 12' clg., 13' clg., up, his w.i.c., shwr., exercise room 14³ x 14⁹ 10' clg., 2-story clg. 23⁴ clg., elev., 12' clg., dn., wet bar, 11' clg., pwdr. bath, stor., theater 17⁴ x 21⁰ 10' clg., up

© eric brown design group, inc.

DESIGN HPT800169

First Floor: 4,661 square feet
Second Floor: 4,178 square feet
Total: 8,839 square feet

Width: 112'-10"
Depth: 92'-8"

Windows highlight the elegance and royalty of this Sun country delight. Three rounded dormers made entirely of windows add delicacy to this gracious facade. French doors are the rule in this home. French doors lead into the foyer through to the parlor, which contains two sets of French doors to the two-story veranda. The study, master suite, guest suites, and all the rooms on the second level showcase French doors. The kitchen is located in a prime position to easily serve the formal dining room. An exercise room and home theater are found along with one guest suite and the master suite on the second level.

A PLACE IN THE SUN

DESIGN HPT800170

First Floor: 3,517 square feet
Second Floor: 1,254 square feet
Total: 4,771 square feet

Width: 95'-8"
Depth: 107'-0"

The design of this Country French estate captures its ambiance with its verandas, grand entry and unique balconies. A spectacular panorama of the formal living areas and the elegant curved monumental stairway awaits just off the raised foyer. A large island kitchen, breakfast nook and family room will impress, as will the breakfast nook and wine cellar. Plenty of kitchen pantry space leads to the laundry and motor court featuring a two-car garage attached to the main house and a three-car garage attached by a breezeway. The master suite boasts a sunken sitting area with a see-through fireplace, His and Hers walk-in closets, island tub and large separate shower. A study area, three additional bedrooms, full bath and a bonus area reside on the second floor.

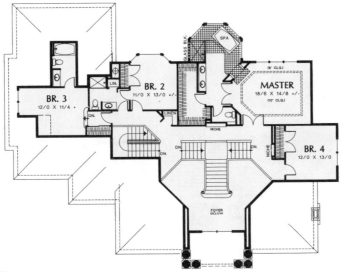

First Floor: 2,342 square feet
Second Floor: 1,597 square feet
Total: 3,939 square feet

Width: 78'-0"
Depth: 62'-0"

Arched windows and a high, arch-top entry complement an unrestrained floor plan in this unique contemporary home. A two-story foyer opens to a stylish, secluded den and to a formal living room with a focal-point fireplace and a coffered ceiling. The U-shaped kitchen contains plenty of counter space and a huge open area for all your cooking needs. The morning nook opens through French doors to a columned, covered deck and leads through graceful arches to the family room. A fireplace and bright windows make the family room enjoyable all year round. Upstairs, a rambling master suite boasts a set of French doors to a lavish bath, complete with a tile-rimmed spa tub, a sizable walk-in closet and twin lavatories.

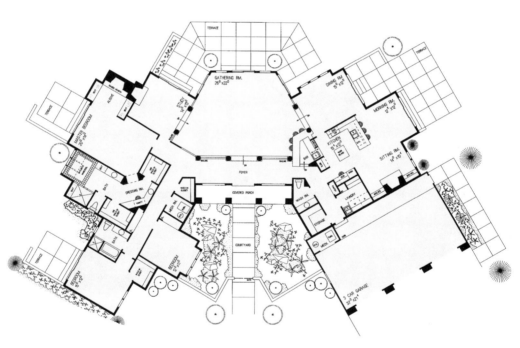

DESIGN HPT800172

Square Footage: 3,505

Width: 110'-7"
Depth: 66'-11"

Loaded with custom features, this plan is designed to delight the imagination. The foyer enters directly into the commanding sunken gathering room. Framed by an elegant railing, this centerpiece for entertaining is open to both the study and the formal dining room, and offers sliding glass doors to the terrace. A full bar further extends the entertaining possibilities of this room. The country-style kitchen contains an efficient work area, as well as a morning room and sitting area—ideal for family gatherings around the cozy fireplace. The grand master suite has a private terrace, fireplace alcove with built-in seats and a huge spa-style bath. Two nicely sized bedrooms and a hall bath round out the plan.

Grand living takes place in this expansive estate. Just beyond the foyer, the living room provides an elegant centerpiece to the floor plan with its soaring ceiling and wall of glass. Flanking the living room are the dining room and study. To the left of the plan, a second foyer gives entry to the opulent master suite. More casual living takes place in the right wing, where the gourmet kitchen adjoins a breakfast nook and a leisure room with a pyramid ceiling and fireplace.

DESIGN HPT800173

First Floor: 3,734 square feet
Second Floor: 418 square feet
Total: 4,152 square feet

Width: 82'-0"
Depth: 107'-0"

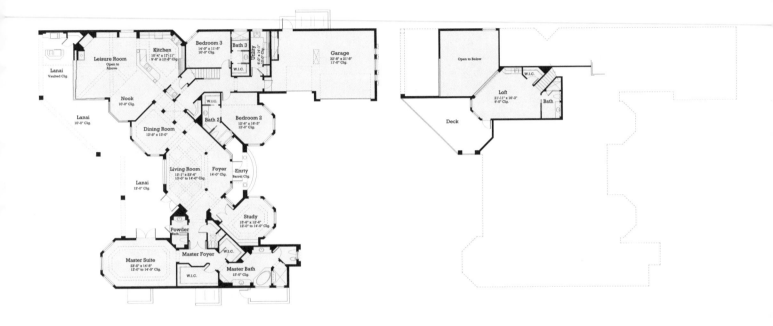

Photo by ©Everett and Soule, courtesy of The Sater Design Collection

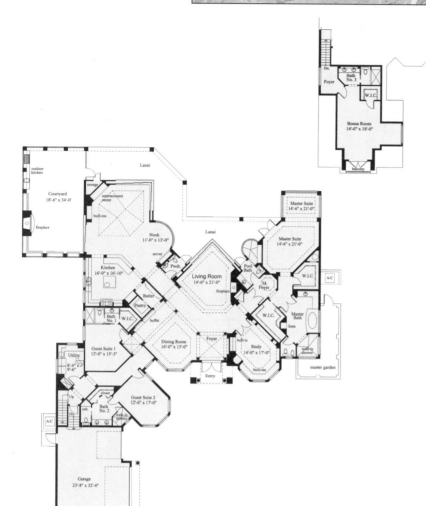

DESIGN HPT800174

Square Footage: 4,604
Bonus Space: 565 square feet
Width: 98'-5"
Depth: 126'-11"

The lavish master suite is the highlight of this grand estate—located in the right wing, it offers a private sitting area, double-door access to the rear lanai, a spacious bath with a step-up tub and walk-in shower, and a large walk-in closet. The home provides many other amenities as well—two guest suites, a study with built-in bookshelves, a formal dining room with space for a buffet table, and a large leisure room with a fireplace and entertainment center. A courtyard, complete with a fireplace and outdoor kitchen, is a great space for outdoor gatherings. Upstairs, an expansive bonus area with a private bath and balcony can serve as guest quarters.

DESIGN HPT800175

First Floor: 3,852 square feet

Second Floor: 903 square feet

Total: 4,755 square feet

Width: 81'-10"
Depth: 104'-0"

Welcome to luxurious living in this opulent Floridian estate. Throughout the interior, distinctive ceiling treatments—coffered, stepped, and slumped-arch—seem to create even more space. The rambling floor plan moves easily between indoors and outdoors—the living room, master suite and leisure room all open to the expansive veranda, which features an outdoor kitchen, and the master bath overlooks a private garden. Five bedrooms are distributed throughout the plan, allowing privacy for everyone; the master suite and two family bedrooms are on the first floor, while two guest suites flank a loft area upstairs. The guests may share in the luxury, as each guest suite includes a private bath and access to a deck.

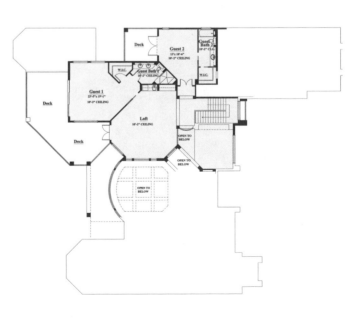

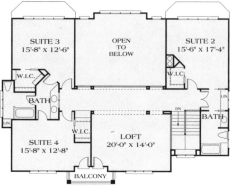

DESIGN HPT800181

First Floor: 2,450 square feet

Second Floor: 1,675 square feet

Total: 4,125 square feet

Finished Basement: 1,568 square feet

Width: 65'-10"

Depth: 85'-2"

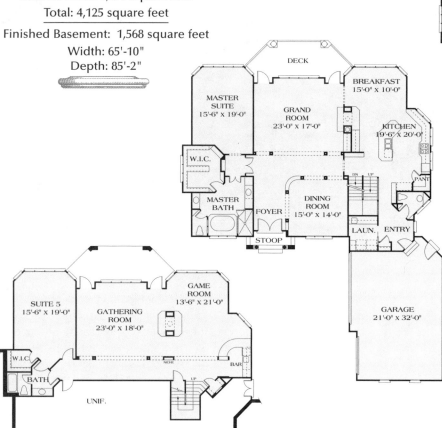

Designed for sloping lots, this magnificent estate home offers windows that overlook the rear grounds from three separate levels. From the first floor, the foyer opens to a spacious dining room and grand room enriched by decorative columns and an abundance of windows. To the right is a large kitchen with an adjacent breakfast nook. The classic master suite claims the remainder of the first floor. Upstairs, three suites and a loft feature opportunities to survey the surrounding landscape. The lower level provides lots of space for family and friends. A gathering room and game room share the warmth of a fireplace and access to a covered patio. An additional suite that's well suited for guests completes the plan.

DESIGN HPT800182

First Floor: 3,307 square feet
Second Floor: 1,642 square feet
Total: 4,949 square feet
Bonus Room: 373 square feet
Width: 132'-6"
Depth: 74'-0"

To truly appreciate this estate, you must go beyond its facade—it's so much more than just another pretty face! The layout is packed with unique features and living areas beyond regular floor planning. Of course, there are all the formal and informal spaces you expect and want: formal living and dining rooms, a casual gathering room and a sunny breakfast room. But this home adds a study or parlor that is flexible enough to suit your needs. The master suite is on the first floor—you've never seen a bath quite like this one! Upstairs are three family bedrooms, plus an immense bonus room with balcony. Don't miss the additional suite over the garage. And there's a pool house that can easily be used as a guest house. It has a fireplace, a full bath and a dressing area.

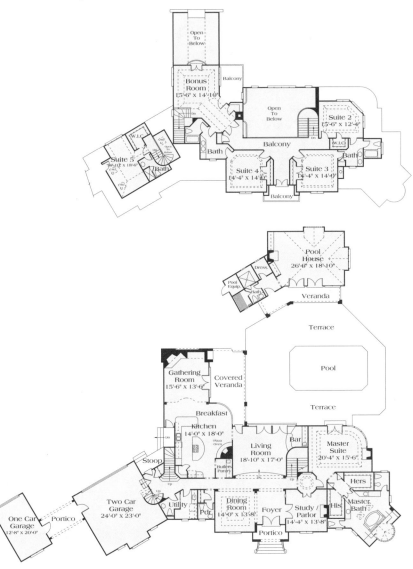

DESIGN HPT800183

First Floor: 2,794 square feet

Second Floor: 1,127 square feet

Total: 3,921 square feet

Width: 85'-0"

Depth: 76'-2"

Elegance is well displayed on this Mediterranean manor by its stone and stucco facade, multi-pane windows, grand entrance and varied rooflines. The grand foyer introduces the formal dining room on the left and a spacious formal living room directly ahead. The study and living room share a through-fireplace, and both have access to the backyard. The kitchen features a walk-in pantry, a cooktop island, a pass-through to the rear veranda, and an adjacent octagonal breakfast nook. Nearby, the leisure room is complete with a coffered ceiling, built-ins and another fireplace. The master suite resides on the right side of the home, and provides two walk-in closets and a lavish bath. Upstairs, two family bedrooms share a bath while a guest suite is designed to pamper visitors.

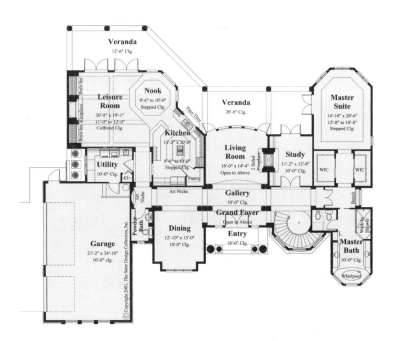

<table>
<tr><td>

editerranean accents enhance the facade of this contemporary estate home. Two fanciful turret bays add a sense of grandeur to the exterior. Double doors open inside to a grand two-story foyer. A two-sided fireplace warms the study and two-story living room. The master suite is found to the right and includes a private bath, two walk-in closets and double-door access to the sweeping rear veranda. Casual areas of the home include the gourmet island kitchen, breakfast nook and leisure room warmed by a fireplace. A spiral staircase leads upstairs, where a second-floor balcony separates two family bedrooms from the luxurious guest suite.

</td></tr>
</table>

DESIGN HPT800184

First Floor: 2,829 square feet
Second Floor: 1,127 square feet
Total: 3,956 square feet

Width: 85'-0"
Depth: 76'-2"

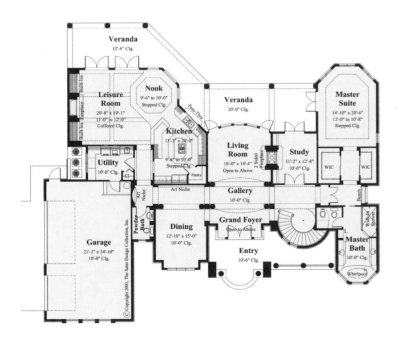

© Copyright 2001, The Sater Design Collection, Inc.

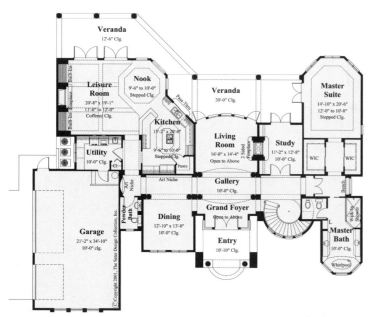

© Copyright 2001, The Sater Design Collection, Inc.

Design HPT800185

First Floor: 2,815 square feet
Second Floor: 1,091 square feet
Total: 3,906 square feet

Width: 85'-0"
Depth: 76'-2"

A wealth of luxurious amenities defines the interior of this Mediterranean home. Stepped ceilings highlight the kitchen, breakfast nook and master suite, while a coffered ceiling enhances the leisure room. The living room—with a wall of windows and two entrances to the rear veranda—shares a two-sided fireplace with the study; a second fireplace warms the leisure room. The master suite features a bath with a whirlpool tub. Upstairs, two family bedrooms and a guest suite each boast walk-in closets and share a balcony that overlooks the living room and foyer. Bedroom 3 and the guest suite each open to a private deck, while Bedroom 2 opens to a balcony.

LET US SHOW YOU OUR HOME BLUEPRINT PACKAGE.

BUILDING A HOME? PLANNING A HOME?

OUR BLUEPRINT PACKAGE HAS NEARLY EVERYTHING YOU NEED TO GET THE JOB DONE RIGHT,

whether you're working on your own or with help from an architect, designer, builder or subcontractors. Each Blueprint Package is the result of many hours of work by licensed architects or professional designers.

QUALITY

Hundreds of hours of painstaking effort have gone into the development of your blueprint plan. Each home has been quality-checked by professionals to insure accuracy and buildability.

VALUE

Because we sell in volume, you can buy professional quality blueprints at a fraction of their development cost. With our plans, your dream home design costs substantially less than the fees charged by architects.

SERVICE

Once you've chosen your favorite home plan, you'll receive fast, efficient service whether you choose to mail or fax your order to us or call us toll free at 1-800-521-6797. After you have received your order, call for customer service toll free 1-888-690-1116.

SATISFACTION

Over 50 years of service to satisfied home plan buyers provide us unparalleled experience and knowledge in producing quality blueprints.

ORDER TOLL FREE 1-800-521-6797

After you've looked over our Blueprint Package and Important Extras, call toll free on our Blueprint Hotline: 1-800-521-6797, for current pricing and availability prior to mailing the order form on page 221. We're ready and eager to serve you. After you have received your order, call for customer service toll free 1-888-690-1116.

Each set of blueprints is an interrelated collection of detail sheets which includes components such as floor plans, interior and exterior elevations, dimensions, cross-sections, diagrams and notations. These sheets show exactly how your house is to be built.

SETS MAY INCLUDE:

FRONTAL SHEET
This artist's sketch of the exterior of the house gives you an idea of how the house will look when built and landscaped. Large floor plans show all levels of the house and provide an overview of your new home's livability, as well as a handy reference for deciding on furniture placement.

FOUNDATION PLANS
This sheet shows the foundation layout including support walls, excavated and unexcavated areas, if any, and foundation notes. If slab construction rather than basement, the plan shows footings and details for a monolithic slab. This page, or another in the set, may include a sample plot plan for locating your house on a building site.

DETAILED FLOOR PLANS
These plans show the layout of each floor of the house. Rooms and interior spaces are carefully dimensioned and keys are given for cross-section details provided later in the plans. The positions of electrical outlets and switches are shown.

HOUSE CROSS-SECTIONS
Large-scale views show sections or cut-aways of the foundation, interior walls, exterior walls, floors, stairways and roof details. Additional cross-sections may show important changes in floor, ceiling or roof heights or the relationship of one level to another. Extremely valuable for construction, these sections show exactly how the various parts of the house fit together.

INTERIOR ELEVATIONS
Many of our drawings show the design and placement of kitchen and bathroom cabinets, laundry areas, fireplaces, bookcases and other built-ins. Little "extras," such as mantelpiece and wainscoting drawings, plus molding sections, provide details that give your home that custom touch.

EXTERIOR ELEVATIONS
These drawings show the front, rear and sides of your house and give necessary notes on exterior materials and finishes. Particular attention is given to cornice detail, brick and stone accents or other finish items that make your home unique.

IMPORTANT EXTRAS TO DO THE JOB RIGHT!

*INTRODUCING IMPORTANT PLANNING AND CONSTRUCTION
AIDS DEVELOPED BY OUR PROFESSIONALS TO HELP YOU
SUCCEED IN YOUR HOME-BUILDING PROJECT*

MATERIALS LIST

*(Note: Because of the diversity
of local building codes, our
Materials List does not include
mechanical materials.)*

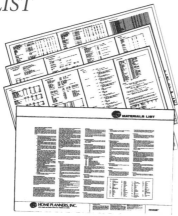

For many of the designs in our portfolio, we offer a customized materials take-off that is invaluable in planning and estimating the cost of your new home. This Materials List outlines the quantity, type and size of materials needed to build your house (with the exception of mechanical system items). Included are framing lumber, windows and doors, kitchen and bath cabinetry, rough and finish hardware, and much more. This handy list helps you or your builder cost out materials and serves as a reference sheet when you're compiling bids. Some Materials Lists may be ordered before blueprints are ordered, call for information.

SPECIFICATION OUTLINE

This valuable 16-page document is critical to building your house correctly. Designed to be filled in by you or your builder, this book lists 166 stages or items crucial to the building process. It provides a comprehensive review of the construction process and helps in choosing materials. When combined with the blueprints, a signed contract, and a schedule, it becomes a legal document and record for the building of your home.

QUOTE ONE®

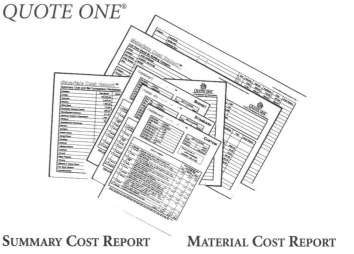

SUMMARY COST REPORT   MATERIAL COST REPORT

A product for estimating the cost of building select designs, the Quote One® system is available in two separate stages: The Summary Cost Report and the Material Cost Report.

The **Summary Cost Report** is the first stage in the package and shows the total cost per square foot for your chosen home in your zip-code area and then breaks that cost down into various categories showing the costs for building materials, labor and installation. The report includes three grades: Budget, Standard and Custom. These reports allow you to evaluate your building budget and compare the costs of building a variety of homes in your area.

Make even more informed decisions about your home-building project with the second phase of our package, our **Material Cost Report.** This tool is invaluable in planning and estimating the cost of your new home. The material and installation (labor and equipment) cost is shown for each of over 1,000 line items provided in the Materials List (Standard grade), which is included when you purchase this estimating tool. It allows you to determine building costs for your specific zip-code area and for your chosen home design. Space is allowed for additional estimates from contractors and subcontractors, such as for mechanical materials, which are not included in our packages. This invaluable tool includes a Materials List. A Material Cost Report cannot be ordered before blueprints are ordered. Call for details. In addition, ask about our Home Planners Estimating Package.

If you are interested in a plan that is not indicated as Quote One®, please call and ask our sales reps. They will be happy to verify the status for you. To order these invaluable reports, use the order form.

CONSTRUCTION INFORMATION

*IF YOU WANT TO KNOW MORE ABOUT TECHNIQUES—
and deal more confidently with subcontractors —
we offer these useful sheets. Each set is an excellent
tool that will add to your understanding of these
technical subjects. These helpful details provide
general construction information and
are not specific to any single plan.*

PLUMBING

The Blueprint Package includes locations for all the plumbing fixtures, including sinks, lavatories, tubs, showers, toilets, laundry trays and water heaters. However, if you want to know more about the complete plumbing system, these Plumbing Details will prove very useful. Prepared to meet requirements of the National Plumbing Code, these fact-filled sheets give general information on pipe schedules, fittings, sump-pump details, water-softener hookups, septic system details and much more. Sheets also include a glossary of terms.

ELECTRICAL

The locations for every electrical switch, plug and outlet are shown in your Blueprint Package. However, these Electrical Details go further to take the mystery out of household electrical systems. Prepared to meet requirements of the National Electrical Code, these comprehensive drawings come packed with helpful information, including wire sizing, switch-installation schematics, cable-routing details, appliance wattage, doorbell hook-ups, typical service panel circuitry and much more. A glossary of terms is also included.

CONSTRUCTION

The Blueprint Package contains information an experienced builder needs to construct a particular house. However, it doesn't show all the ways that houses can be built, nor does it explain alternate construction methods. To help you understand how your house will be built—and offer additional techniques—this set of Construction Details depicts the materials and methods used to build foundations, fireplaces, walls, floors and roofs. Where appropriate, the drawings show acceptable alternatives.

MECHANICAL

These Mechanical Details contain fundamental principles and useful data that will help you make informed decisions and communicate with subcontractors about heating and cooling systems. Drawings contain instructions and samples that allow you to make simple load calculations, and preliminary sizing and costing analysis. Covered are the most commonly used systems from heat pumps to solar fuel systems. The package is filled with illustrations and diagrams to help you visualize components and how they relate to one another.

THE HANDS-ON HOME FURNITURE PLANNER

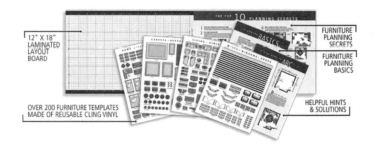

Effectively plan the space in your home using The **Hands-On Home Furniture Planner**. It's fun and easy—no more moving heavy pieces of furniture to see how the room will go together. And you can try different layouts, moving furniture at a whim.

The kit includes reusable peel and stick furniture templates that fit onto a 12" x 18" laminated layout board—space enough to layout every room in your home.

Also included in the package are a number of helpful planning tools. You'll receive:

✓ Helpful hints and solutions for difficult situations.
✓ Furniture planning basics to get you started.
✓ Furniture planning secrets that let you in on some of the tricks of professional designers.

The **Hands-On Home Furniture Planner** is the one tool that no new homeowner or home remodeler should be without. It's also a perfect housewarming gift!

To Order, Call Toll Free 1-800-521-6797

After you've looked over our Blueprint Package and Important Extras on these pages, call for current pricing and availability prior to mailing the order form. We're ready and eager to serve you. After you have received your order, call for customer service toll free 1-888-690-1116.

Purchase Policy

Accurate construction-cost estimates should come from your builder after review of the construction drawings. Your purchase includes a license to use the plans to construct one single-family residence. You may not use this design to build a second or derivative work, or construct multiple dwellings without purchasing another set of drawings or paying additional design fees. An additional identical set of the same plan in the same order may be purchased within a 60-day period at $50 per set, plus shipping and sales tax. After 60 days, re-orders are treated as new orders.

Sepias, vellums and other reproducibles are not refundable, returnable or exchangeable. Reproducible vellums are granted with a non-exclusive license to do the following:

- ❏ to modify the drawings for use in the construction of a single home.
- ❏ to make up to twelve (12) copies of the plans for use in the construction of a single home.
- ❏ to construct one and only one home based on the plans, either in the original form or as modified by you.

Plans were designed to meet the requirements of the local building codes in the jurisdiction for which they were drawn. Because codes are subject to various changes and interpretations, the purchaser is responsible for compliance with all local building codes, ordinances, site conditions, subdivision restrictions and structural elements by having their builder review the plans to ensure compliance. We strongly recommend that an engineer in your area review your plans before you apply for a permit or actual construction begins. We authorize the use of our drawings on the express condition that you strictly comply with all local building codes, zoning requirements and other applicable laws, regulations, ordinances and requirements.

INDEX

To use the Index at the right, refer to the design number (a helpful page reference is also given).
TO ORDER: Fill in and send the order form on page 221 or, if you prefer, fax to 1-800-224-6699 or call toll free 1-800-521-6797.

Plans Price Schedule
Prices guaranteed through December 31, 2002

One-set Building Package

One set of vellum construction drawings plus one set of study blueprints @ $.35/square foot

Eight-set Blueprint Pack:
$.30 square foot

Additional Set of Identical Blueprints in same order
(must be ordered within 60 days of original purchase):
$50 set

Specification Outlines:
$10 each

Materials List are available for many designers:
call for pricing

PLAN INDEX

PLAN INDEX

BEFORE FILLING OUT THE ORDER FORM, PLEASE CALL US ON OUR TOLL-FREE BLUEPRINT HOTLINE 1-800-521-6797. YOU MAY WANT TO LEARN MORE ABOUT OUR SERVICES AND PRODUCTS. HERE'S SOME INFORMATION YOU WILL FIND HELPFUL.

OUR EXCHANGE POLICY

With the exception of reproducible plan orders, we will exchange your entire first order for an equal or greater number of blueprints within our plan collection within 90 days of the original order. The entire content of your original order must be returned before an exchange will be processed. Please call our customer service department for your return authorization number and shipping instructions. If the returned blueprints look used, redlined or copied, we will not honor your exchange. Fees for exchanging your blueprints are as follows: 20% of the amount of the original order...plus the difference in cost if exchanging for a design in a higher price bracket or less the difference in cost if exchanging for a design in a lower price bracket. **(Reproducible blueprints are not exchangeable or refundable.)** Please call for current postage and handling prices. Shipping and handling charges are not refundable.

ABOUT REPRODUCIBLES

When purchasing a reproducible you may be required to furnish a fax number. The designer will fax documents that you must sign and return to them before shipping will take place.

ABOUT REVERSE BLUEPRINTS

Although lettering and dimensions will appear backward, reverses will be a useful aid if you decide to flop the plan. See Price Schedule and Plans Index for pricing.

REVISING, MODIFYING AND CUSTOMIZING PLANS

Like many homeowners who buy these plans, you and your builder, architect or engineer may want to make changes to them. We recommend purchase of a reproducible plan for any changes made by your builder, licensed architect or engineer. As set forth below, we cannot assume any responsibility for blueprints which have been changed, whether by you, your builder or by professionals selected by you or referred to you by us, because such individuals are outside our supervision and control.

ARCHITECTURAL AND ENGINEERING SEALS

Some cities and states are now requiring that a licensed architect or engineer review and "seal" a blueprint, or officially approve it, prior to construction due to concerns over energy costs, safety and other factors. Prior to application for a building permit or the start of actual construction, we strongly advise that you consult your local building official who can tell you if such a review is required.

ABOUT THE DESIGNS

The architects and designers whose work appears in this publication are among America's leading residential designers. Each plan was designed to meet the requirements of a nationally recognized model building code in effect at the time and place the plan was drawn. Because national building codes change from time to time, plans may not comply with any such code at the time they are sold to a customer. In addition, building officials may not accept these plans as final construction documents of record as the plans may need to be modified and additional drawings and details added to suit local conditions and requirements. We strongly advise that purchasers consult a licensed architect or engineer, and their local building official, before starting any construction related to these plans.

LOCAL BUILDING CODES AND ZONING REQUIREMENTS

At the time of creation, our plans are drawn to specifications published by the Building Officials and Code Administrators (BOCA) International, Inc.; the Southern Building Code Congress (SBCCI) International, Inc.; the International Conference of Building Officials (ICBO); or the Council of American Building Officials (CABO). Our plans are designed to meet or exceed national building standards. Because of the great differences in geography and climate throughout the United States and Canada, each state, county and municipality has its own building codes, zone requirements, ordinances and building regulations. Your plan may need to be modified to comply with local requirements regarding snow loads, energy codes, soil and seismic conditions and a wide range of other matters. In addition, you may need to obtain permits or inspections from local governments before and in the course of construction. Prior to using blueprints ordered from us, we strongly advise that you consult a licensed architect or engineer—and speak with your local building official—before applying for any permit or beginning construction. We authorize the use of our blueprints on the express condition that you strictly comply with all local building codes, zoning requirements and other applicable laws, regulations, ordinances and requirements. Notice: Plans for homes to be built in Nevada must be re-drawn by a Nevada-registered professional. Consult your building official for more information on this subject.

TOLL FREE
1-800-521-6797

REGULAR OFFICE HOURS:
8:00 a.m.-9:00 p.m. EST,
Monday-Friday

If we receive your order by 3:00 p.m. EST, Monday-Friday, we'll process it and ship within **two business days**. When ordering by phone, please have your credit card or check information ready. We'll also ask you for the Order Form Key Number at the bottom of the order form.

By FAX: Copy the Order Form on the next page and send it on our FAX line: 1-800-224-6699 or 520-544-3086.

Canadian Customers
Order Toll Free 1-877-223-6389

DISCLAIMER

The designers we work with have put substantial care and effort into the creation of their blueprints. However, because they cannot provide on-site consultation, supervision and control over actual construction, and because of the great variance in local building requirements, building practices and soil, seismic, weather and other conditions, WE CANNOT MAKE ANY WARRANTY, EXPRESS OR IMPLIED, WITH RESPECT TO THE CONTENT OR USE OF THE BLUEPRINTS, INCLUDING BUT NOT LIMITED TO ANY WARRANTY OF MERCHANTABILITY OR OF FITNESS FOR A PARTICULAR PURPOSE. **ITEMS, PRICES, TERMS AND CONDITIONS ARE SUBJECT TO CHANGE WITHOUT NOTICE. REPRODUCIBLE PLAN ORDERS MAY REQUIRE A CUSTOMER'S SIGNED RELEASE BEFORE SHIPPING.**

TERMS AND CONDITIONS

These designs are protected under the terms of United States Copyright Law and may not be copied or reproduced in any way, by any means, unless you have purchased Reproducibles which clearly indicate your right to copy or reproduce. We authorize the use of your chosen design as an aid in the construction of one single family home only. You may not use this design to build a second or multiple dwellings without purchasing another blueprint or blueprints or paying additional design fees.

HOW MANY BLUEPRINTS DO YOU NEED?

Although a standard building package may satisfy many states, cities and counties, some plans may require certain changes. For your convenience, we have developed a Reproducible plan which allows a local professional to modify and make up to 10 copies of your revised plan. As our plans are all copyright protected, with your purchase of the Reproducible, we will supply you with a Copyright release letter. The number of copies you may need: 1 for owner; 3 for builder; 2 for local building department and 1-3 sets for your mortgage lender.

ORDER TOLL FREE!

For information about any of our services or to order call
1-800-521-6797

Browse our website:
www.eplans.com

BLUEPRINTS ARE NOT REFUNDABLE EXCHANGES ONLY

For Customer Service, call toll free
1-888-690-1116.

HOME PLANNERS, LLC
Wholly owned by Hanley-Wood, LLC
3275 WEST INA ROAD, SUITE 110
TUCSON, ARIZONA 85741

THE BASIC PACKAGE

Rush me the following (Please refer to the Plans Index and Price Schedule on page 218-219):
One-Set Building Package for Plan Number(s)@ $.35/sq. ft._____. $_____
___ Eight-set Blueprint Package @ $.30/sq. ft. $_____
___ Additional Identical Blueprints in same order @$50 per set $_____

ADDITIONAL PRODUCTS

Rush me the following:
___ Home Furniture Planner @ $15.95 ea. $_____
___ Specification Outlines @ $10 each. $_____
___ Materials List call for pricing and availability. $_____
___ Detail Sets @$14.95 each; any two for $22.95; any three for $29.95; all four for $39.95 (Save $19.85). $_____
    ___Plumbing___Electrical___Construction___Mechanical
(These helpful details provide general construction advice and are not specific to any single plan.)

POSTAGE AND HANDLING	1-3 sets	4 or more sets
Signature is required for all deliveries.		
Delivery: (No COD's)		
(Requires street address—No P.o. Boxes)		
• Regular Service (Allow 7-10 business days delivery)	$20.00	$25.00
• Priority (Allow 4-5 business days delivery)	$25.00	$35.00
• Express (Allow 3 business days delivery)	$35.00	$45.00
OVERSEAS DELIVERY: Fax, phone or mail for quote.		
NOTE: All delivery times are from date Construction Drawings are shipped.		

POSTAGE (From box above) $_____
SUBTOTAL $_____
SALES TAX (AZ & MI residents please add appropriate state & local sales tax.) $_____
TOTAL (Subtotal and Tax) $_____

YOUR ADDRESS (Please print legibly)

Name _____

Street _____

City_____State_____Zip_____

Daytime telephone number (required)(____) _____

TeleCheck® Checks By Phone℠ available

FOR CREDIT CARD ORDERS ONLY

Please fill in the information below:
Credit card number _____

Exp. Date: Month/Year _____
Check one ❑ Visa   ❑ MasterCard   ❑ Discover   ❑ American Express

Signature (required)_____
Please check appropriate box: ❑ Licensed Builder-Contractor
        ❑ Homeowner

BY FAX: Copy the order form above and send it on our FAXLINE: **1-800-224-6699 or 520-544-3086**

Order Form Key

HPT80

1 BIGGEST & BEST

1001 of our best-selling plans in one volume. 1,074 to 7,275 square feet. 704 pgs $12.95 1K1

2 ONE-STORY

450 designs for all lifestyles. 800 to 4,900 square feet. 384 pgs $9.95 OS

3 MORE ONE-STORY

475 superb one-level plans from 800 to 5,000 square feet. 448 pgs $9.95 MO2

4 TWO-STORY

443 designs for one-and-a-half and two stories. 1,500 to 6,000 square feet. 448 pgs $9.95 TS

5 VACATION

430 designs for recreation, retirement and leisure. 448 pgs $9.95 VS3

6 HILLSIDE

208 designs for split-levels, bi-levels, multi-levels and walkouts. 224 pgs $9.95 HH

7 FARMHOUSE

300 Fresh Designs from Classic to Modern. 320 pgs. $10.95 FCP

8 COUNTRY HOUSES

208 unique home plans that combine traditional style and modern livability. 224 pgs $9.95 CN

9 BUDGET-SMART

200 efficient plans from 7 top designers, that you can really afford to build! 224 pgs $8.95 BS

10 BARRIER-FREE

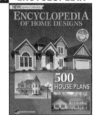

Over 1,700 products and 51 plans for accessible living. 128 pgs $15.95 UH

11 ENCYCLOPEDIA

500 exceptional plans for all styles and budgets—the best book of its kind! 528 pgs $9.95 ENC

12 ENCYCLOPEDIA II

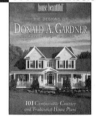

500 completely new plans. Spacious and stylish designs for every budget and taste. 352 pgs $9.95 E2

13 AFFORDABLE

300 Modest plans for savvy homebuyers.256 pgs. $9.95 AH2

14 VICTORIAN

210 striking Victorian and Farmhouse designs from today's top designers. 224 pgs $15.95 VDH2

15 ESTATE

Dream big! Eighteen designers showcase their biggest and best plans. 224 pgs $16.95 EDH3

16 LUXURY

170 lavish designs, over 50% brand-new plans added to a most elegant collection. 192 pgs $12.95 LD3

17 EUROPEAN STYLES

200 homes with a unique flair of the Old World. 224 pgs $15.95 EURO

18 COUNTRY CLASSICS

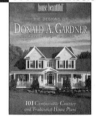

Donald Gardner's 101 best Country and Traditional home plans. 192 pgs $17.95 DAG

19 COUNTRY

85 Charming Designs from American Home Gallery. 160 pgs. $17.95 CTY

20 TRADITIONAL

85 timeless designs from the Design Traditions Library. 160 pgs. $17.95 TRA

21 COTTAGES

245 Delightful retreats from 825 to 3,500 square feet. 256 pgs. $10.95 COOL

22 CABINS TO VILLAS

Enchanting Homes for Mountain Sea or Sun, from the Sater collection. 144 pgs $19.95 CCV

23 CONTEMPORARY

The most complete and imaginative collection of contemporary designs available anywhere. 256 pgs. $10.95 CM2

24 FRENCH COUNTRY

Live every day in the French countryside using these plans, landscapes and interiors. 192 pgs $14.95 PN

25 SOUTHERN

207 homes rich in Southern styling and comfort. 240 pgs $8.95 SH

26 SOUTHWESTERN

138 designs that capture the spirit of the Southwest. 144 pgs $10.95 SW

27 SHINGLE-STYLE

155 Home plans from Classic Colonials to Breezy Bungalows. 192 pgs. $12.95 SNG

28 NEIGHBORHOOD

170 designs with the feel of main street America. 192 pgs $12.95 TND

29 CRAFTSMAN

170 Home plans in the Craftsman and Bungalow style. 192 pgs $12.95 CC

30 GRAND VISTAS

200 Homes with a View. 224 pgs. $10.95 GV

Home Planners wants your building experience to be as pleasant and trouble-free as possible.
That's why we've expanded our library of do-it-yourself titles to help you along.

31 DUPLEX & TOWNHOMES

115 Duplex, Multiplex &
Townhome Designs. 128 pgs.
$17.95 MFH

32 WATERFRONT

200 designs perfect for your
waterside wonderland.
208 pgs $10.95 WF

33 NATURAL LIGHT

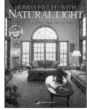

223 Sunny home plans for all
regions. 240 pgs. $8.95 NA

34 NOSTALGIA

100 Time-Honored designs
updated with today's features.
224 pgs. $14.95 NOS

35 STREET OF DREAMS

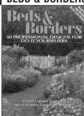

Over 300 photos showcase
54 prestigious homes.
256 pgs $19.95 SOD

36 NARROW-LOT

250 Designs for houses
17' to 50' wide. 256 pgs.
$9.95 NL2

37 SMALL HOUSES

Innovative plans for
sensible lifestyles.
224 pgs. $8.95 SM2

38 GARDENS & MORE

225 gardens, landscapes,
decks and more to
enhance every home.
320 pgs. $19.95 GLP

39 EASY-CARE

41 special landscapes
designed for beauty and
low maintenance.
160 pgs $14.95 ECL

40 BACKYARDS

40 designs focused solely on
creating your own specially
themed backyard oasis. 160
pgs $14.95 BYL

41 BEDS & BORDERS

40 Professional designs
for do-it-yourselfers.
160 pgs. $14.95 BB

42 BUYER'S GUIDE

A comprehensive look at 2700
products for all aspects of
landscaping & gardening.
128 pgs $19.95 LPBG

43 OUTDOOR

74 easy-to-build designs,
lets you create and build
your own backyard oasis.
128 pgs $9.95 YG2

44 GARAGES

145 exciting projects from
64 to 1,900 square feet.
160 pgs. $9.95 GG2

45 DECKS

A brand new collection
of 120 beautiful and
practical decks. 144 pgs.
$9.95 DP2

46 HOME BUILDING

Everything you need to know
to work with contractors and
subcontractors. 212 pgs
$14.95 HBP

47 RURAL BUILDING

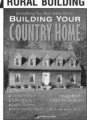

Everything you need to know
to build your home in the
country. 232 pgs.
$14.95 BYC

48 VACATION HOMES

Your complete guide to
building your vacation
home. 224 pgs.
$14.95 BYV

LANDSCAPE DESIGNS

PROJECT GUIDES

- -

Book Order Form

To order your books, just check the box of the book numbered below and complete the coupon. We will process
your order and ship it from our office within two business days. Send coupon and check (in U.S. funds).

YES! Please send me the books I've indicated:

- ❏ 1:1K1 ....$12.95
- ❏ 2:OS $9.95
- ❏ 3:MO2 ....$9.95
- ❏ 4:TS $9.95
- ❏ 5:VS3 ....$9.95
- ❏ 6:HH $9.95
- ❏ 7:FCP $10.95
- ❏ 8:CN $9.95
- ❏ 9:BS $8.95
- ❏ 10:UH $15.95
- ❏ 11:ENC........$9.95
- ❏ 12:E2 ....$9.95
- ❏ 13:AH2.........$9.95
- ❏ 14:VDH2 ....$15.95
- ❏ 15:EDH3 ...$16.95
- ❏ 16:LD3 ......$12.95

- ❏ 17:EURO ...$15.95
- ❏ 18:DAG $17.95
- ❏ 19:CTY $17.95
- ❏ 20:TRA $17.95
- ❏ 21:COOL ...$10.95
- ❏ 22:CCV $19.95
- ❏ 23:CM2 .....$10.95
- ❏ 24:PN $14.95
- ❏ 25:SH $8.95
- ❏ 26:SW $10.95
- ❏ 27:SNG $12.95
- ❏ 28:TND $12.95
- ❏ 29:CC $12.95
- ❏ 30:GV $10.95
- ❏ 31:MFH.....$17.95
- ❏ 32:WF $10.95

- ❏ 33:NA..........$8.95
- ❏ 34:NOS $14.95
- ❏ 35:SOD $19.95
- ❏ 36:NL2 ....$9.95
- ❏ 37:SM2 ....$8.95
- ❏ 38:GLP......$19.95
- ❏ 39:ECL $14.95
- ❏ 40:BYL $14.95
- ❏ 41:BB $14.95
- ❏ 42:LPBG $19.95
- ❏ 43:YG2 ....$9.95
- ❏ 44:GG2 ....$9.95
- ❏ 45:DP2........$9.95
- ❏ 46:HBP $14.95
- ❏ 47:BYC......$14.95
- ❏ 48:BYV......$14.95

Canadian Customers Order Toll Free 1-877-223-6389

Books Subtotal $_____
ADD Postage and Handling (allow 4–6 weeks for delivery) $ 4.00
Sales Tax: (AZ & MI residents, add state and local sales tax.) $_____
YOUR TOTAL (Subtotal, Postage/Handling, Tax) $_____

YOUR ADDRESS (PLEASE PRINT)

Name _____

Street _____

City _____ State _____ Zip _____

Phone (_____) _____ — _____

YOUR PAYMENT

TeleCheck® Checks By Phone℠ available
Check one: ❏ Check ❏ Visa ❏ MasterCard ❏ Discover ❏ American Express
Required credit card information:

Credit Card Number _____

Expiration Date (Month/Year)_____ / _____

Signature Required _____

Home Planners, LLC
3275 W. Ina Road, Suite 110, Dept. BK, Tucson, AZ 85741

HPT80

FOR FASTER SERVICE ORDER ONLINE AT
www.hwspecials.com

HEAT-N-GLO
1-888-427-3973
WWW.HEATNGLO.COM

Heat-N-Glo offers quality gas, woodburning and electric fireplaces, including gas log sets, stoves, and inserts for preexisting fireplaces. Now available gas grills and outdoor fireplaces. Send for a free brochure.

Ideas for your next project. Beautiful, durable, elegant low-maintenance millwork, mouldings, balustrade systems and much more. For your free catalog please call us at 1-800-446-3040 or visit www.stylesolutionsinc.com.

ARISTOKRAFT
ONE MASTERBRAND CABINETS DRIVE
JASPER, IN 47546
(812) 482-2527
WWW.ARISTOKRAFT.COM

Aristokraft offers you superb value, outstanding quality and great style that fit your budget. Transform your great ideas into reality with popular styles and features that reflect your taste and lifestyle. $5.00

THERMA-TRU DOORS
1687 WOODLANDS DRIVE
MAUMEE, OH 43537
1-800-THERMA-TRU
WWW.THERMATRU.COM

The undisputed brand leader, Therma-Tru specializes in fiberglass and steel entry doors for every budget. Excellent craftsmanship, energy efficiency and variety make Therma-Tru the perfect choice for all your entry door needs.

225 GARDEN, LANDSCAPE
AND PROJECT PLANS
TO ORDER, CALL
1-800-322-6797

225 Do-It-Yourself designs that help transform boring yards into exciting outdoor entertainment spaces. Gorgeous gardens, luxurious landscapes, dazzling decks and other outdoor amenities. Complete construction blueprints available for every project. Only $19.95 (plus $4 shipping/handling).

HAVE WE GOT PLANS FOR YOU!

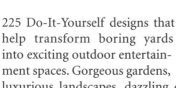

Your online source for home designs and ideas. Find thousands of plans from the nation's top designers...all in one place. Plus, links to the best known names in building supplies and services.